The
·Llewellyn·
Tarot Companion

About Anna-Marie Ferguson

The creator of the popular *Legend: The Arthurian Tarot*, Anna-Marie Ferguson is a self-taught artist whose passion for history and legend led her to paint and, later, to write about its characters and dramas. Over the years, her paintings of these classical subjects have served as both book illustrations and works of art exhibited in museums and sold through galleries. A member of the international Arthurian Society and the Pendragon Society, she has made numerous television appearances, tours, and lectures on the art of illustration and the Arthurian world.

The Llewellyn
TAROT COMPANION

Anna-Marie Ferguson

Llewellyn Publications
Woodbury, Minnesota

FIRST EDITION
Second Printing, 2006

Book design and editing by Rebecca Zins
Cover and interior art © 2006 by Anna-Marie Ferguson
Cover design by Lisa Novak

Llewellyn is a registered trademark of Llewellyn Worldwide, Ltd.

ISBN-13: 978-0-7387-0299-5
ISBN-10: 0-7387-0299-4
This book is a component of The Llewellyn Tarot kit, which consists of a boxed set of 78 full-color cards, a sheer golden beaded brocade tarot bag, and this perfect-bound book.

Llewellyn Publications
A Division of Llewellyn Worldwide, Ltd.
2143 Wooddale Drive, Dept. 0-7387-0299-4
Woodbury, MN 55125-2989, U.S.A.
www.llewellyn.com

Printed in the United States of America

Contents

Acknowledgments

I am deeply grateful to Christine Mactavish, who has lent her skills in typing two manuscripts: the first to accompany *Legend: The Arthurian Tarot* and herewith *The Llewellyn Tarot*. Ever good-humoured and generous with her time, I count her friendship a blessing.

My thanks to Garth Clarke and Michael Cichon for proofing the manuscript and sharing my love and enthusiasm for things ancient and Welsh. Large, dual-natured projects such as this can be likened to an ocean liner requiring numerous hands and eyes to bring into dock—thank you to Debra Rudolph and Laurie Simpson for their eyes, and to publisher Carl Llewellyn Weschcke for calm, warm seas.

Welsh landscape photographer and author Anthony Griffiths has been very kind in providing inspiring images of the mountain of Cadair Idris and allowing me to paint his view—I much appreciate his help in reaching the summit.

Lastly, my gratitude to Cheryl Leach and Bernice Smithman for their years of practical help, and Brian Demchuk, who as a considerate prairie boy gave me a special chair in which to write this book—a comfortable old chair to match the one in which Zane Grey wrote his "duster" novels.

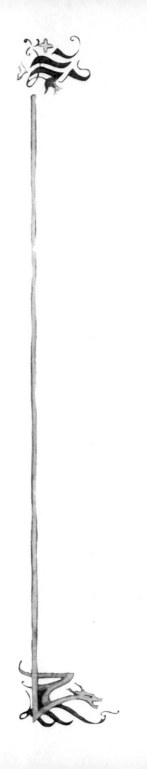

Foreword

Long, long ago, in a place far, far away—in Swansea, Wales—a young boy set out on a journey that took him to America, the land of promise, where he became a well-known astrologer and theosophist. He was the founder of Llewellyn Publications, and some would say he was my spiritual grandfather.

Llewellyn George was born in Swansea on August 17, 1876, at 4:15 AM. He immigrated to America as a young boy by himself. I can well imagine the friends and family he left behind telling him he was embarking on a fool's journey.

I can imagine him thinking, "Better a fool than a solid dullard for whom every day is the same as every other day." He was a Leo, after all, and every important move the company he founded has made has happened with the Sun in the zodiacal sign of Leo.

Most tarot decks show the Fool as rather lackadaisically setting off, smelling the roses and seemingly unaware that he is about to step off a cliff. A fool indeed! The interpretation is that we start our journey into life totally unconscious of the challenges before us.

But look at the Fool in *The Llewellyn Tarot* deck and see instead a youth on a white horse deliberately leaping across the rainbow chasm between the worlds to journey into this land of promise, this world where we live to learn and grow and to become more than we were. Oh, he may be a fool, but he is not foolish. He is filled with courage and purpose, and he is in search of adventure; not a fool's journey, then, but one of heroism.

Our artist, Anna-Marie Ferguson, immersed herself in the history and mythology of Wales—the land of mists and mysteries—in order to produce this new tarot. But it is not "archaic"; rather, it is a true picture-book of the Mysteries themselves. It is a tool offering insight into the Mystery that is life and the Mystery that is the entire universe within which all have being.

Here is the story of the youth who eagerly enters into life, whose first step is that of the Magician. We are born with inner power and knowledge, and our journey is one of discovery and mastery in order to fulfill the promise with which we are born.

The tarot is the Book of Life for those willing to lay it out for revelation and guidance, and then to use its archetypal energies with wisdom and purpose to win at the Game of Life.

This tarot is not only a fortunetelling device but one that is fortune-*making*. These are cards of power that when so used will awaken circuits of energy, represented by their relationships in the formulas you create with your layouts or by any single card you choose with purpose.

Look at the Magician, then the Priestess, then each of the other cards; feel the timeless stirring of their secret (archetypal) energies in your soul. Let them whisper secrets to you, and then speak them into manifestation. Each card has a story to tell, and put into relationships with each other they make new stories that can become reality in this world.

The tarot is the universe hidden in a secret book of cards. That universe is both "out there" and "in here." As above, so below. *The Llewellyn Tarot* deck is the result of five years of intense study and creation by this artist, already knowledgeable and well-known for her creation of *Legend: The Arthurian Tarot* and for her illustrations to the Cassell edition of *Le Morte D'Arthur* edited by John Matthews.

Anna-Marie Ferguson created *The Llewellyn Tarot* to exemplify the very *raison d'être* of Llewellyn as "bringer of light." Llewellyn is named for Llew Llaw Gyffes—"the bright one of the skillful hand"—hero of the *Mabinogion*. He is a solar deity, and his festival is celebrated August 1. He is the essence of zodiacal Leo, as was Llewellyn George, who founded Llewellyn Publications in 1901 and was called "Llew" by his friends.

Llewellyn George wrote seventeen books on astrology and became its leading exponent—writing, publishing, teaching, speaking, and working to spread knowledge and understanding of what I've called "esoteric technology."

When I was a young student, I took a magical name, Gnosticus (Seeker of Knowledge), and when I became a publisher I determined that I would be a Builder of Bridges for people to cross over the chasm of ignorance to knowledge. And that is how I see *The Llewellyn Tarot*—a bridge between the worlds, a revealer of knowledge, an instrument of transformation.

Carl Llewellyn Weschcke

PUBLISHER, LLEWELLYN WORLDWIDE

Preface

Snowdon is the highest mountain in Wales, and on my last visit it was hidden in mist, creating an atmosphere to conjure legends and hold back time. Standing on the summit, one cannot help but imagine the historical figures who have stood on the same rock. And when watching the mist thread through one's fingers, one may be reminded of the red dragon, who heralds the spirit of Wales.

Wales has long been known as the land of enchantment. The wild and remote landscapes fire the imagination and resurrect legendary heroes and medieval histories. Here nature is the enchanter, who with tricks of light and veils of mist will conjure water women to glide on the surface of a lake. Likewise, the play of falling shadows can make one see a battle tail slide through a mountain pass.

The Dark Age and medieval time periods have fascinated me for many years. It is an interest which likely stems from the early influence of a childhood in the New Forest of southern England, which is home to ancient woodlands of beech and oak and wild, open heath that encourage the imagination. The tarot became an interest of mine as a young teenager, with the art being the initial attraction.

Beyond the cards themselves, the tarot introduced me to new concepts, structure, and a poetic language through which I could filter higher thought. I vividly remember the exhilaration of being exposed to new, expanding philosophies by way of the compact tarot, which seemed to have an unending number of orbiting associations in literature and visionary art. A powerful intersection occurs where the virtues, archetypal characters, and dramas of the tarot meet with their mythological counterparts.

As a young illustrator and author, my first large project was *Legend: The Arthurian Tarot*, which drew upon the legend of King Arthur and the Dark Age history of Britain. Having travelled the royal road of the tarot once before, I thought it unlikely to pass that way again. Yet, when Llewellyn Publications proposed this tarot as a special project—to draw on Welsh mythology in deference to the Welsh name of the publishing house—I was given cause to reconsider, and then agree. In my choice of projects, above all other considerations, it has been my mission to re-introduce the old, lesser-known legends to a wider audience and thus contribute in my own small way to their future health as "living legends." When done with care and in good faith, the marriage of a tarot deck and mythology can benefit both traditions. I am honoured to have been asked to create a work to bear the name of its publishing house, Llewellyn, and am most pleased to be in the service of the red dragon.

Wales, Land of the Red Dragon

The enchanted land of Wales lies on the western border of England, and while part of the United Kingdom, it remains a distinct country with its own culture, language, and tradition. It is a land rich in legend, landscape, and the imagination of its Celtic people. The southern regions are green and gentle with feminine hills and fairy vales, while the north is heavy in atmosphere, guarded by old heroic ghosts and mountain grandeur. The land itself seems to breathe an air of enchantment through mist and caves, lakes and waterfalls, and it has long been known as a place of inspiration for artists and writers. Along its rugged coastline lie numerous small and mysterious islands heavy with mist and further histories and legend. Wales was the home of Myrddin, the historical bard who gave rise to the character of Merlin. The great sixth-century poet Taliesin was also a native son, and the inherent love of words and poetry continues to thrive in Wales today. The Welsh language used in this book may seem strange at first, but may be seen as "wondrous strange" when appreciating its age and mystique.

Wales has a proud and turbulent history. On its northwestern tip, *Yns Mons*, Isle of Anglesey, which is a short distance from the northern mainland, was once called *Monmam Cymru*—"mother of Wales"—and is renowned for its ancient monuments and traces of occupation that reach back to the Mesolithic period of 8000–4000 BC. The isle was once the seat of power for the druids of western Europe, who stood defiant on its shore in face of the Roman occupation. After the Roman withdrawal from Britain in the early fifth century, the native Celts, with a somewhat Romanized nobility, established their own administrative system. It was a precarious time of transition, as lesser kings vied for power. Saxons, Angles, and Jutes soon set ashore thinking to take the fertile island for themselves. It was this period of time, around the year 500, when Britain battled numerous invaders, that gave rise to legends of heroes such as King Arthur and Ambrosius. Eventually, the native Britons were pushed back by the aggressors into the western region of the island, now known as Wales, where their culture became the root and foundation of the modern-day Welsh. In legend, the standard of King Arthur and his father, Uther, was the red dragon, which remains the proud national emblem of Wales today. It would seem, however, that the land's association with the red dragon predates the Arthurian Dark Ages and is a tradition stretching back so far as to be lost in the Celtic dawn. The dragon is evocative of the country's heroic nature, which continued to simmer, rise up, and drive the lives of native heroes such as Llewellyn ap Gruffydd and Owain Glyndwr. The many castles of Wales stand as testament to this rebellious spirit; while the castles are loved today for their magnificence, they were built by the English as strongholds of repression in the effort to quell the independent spirit of the Welsh.

Landscape and history aside, Wales is a treasure for its cultural artistic heritage. A small book such as this can only give brief introductions, and the literary legacy of Wales is long and complex, with venerable bards and poets a study unto themselves (see the bibliography to further investigate the riches of Wales). The major arcana of this deck draws upon the early mythology of Wales from medieval sources, traditional quasi-historical legend, and, occasionally, comparatively modern folklore. The Welsh tales can be wildly imaginative, unpredictable, and full of character—here we find a bristling wild boar named Twrch Trwyth, who would rather face death than, as he says, "part with the precious things that lie between my ears!"—these being a comb, razor, and scissors. The moods of the Welsh move from humour, heroics, and love to the sad, silky stories surrounding lakes or the sublime visions of drowned cities and the early, violent versions of the Grail quest. There is a challenge in working with Welsh myths and legends in that so much of these are lost to modern-day readers. Welsh was an oral tradition, passed on through generations of bards who memorized a vast repertoire of cycling sagas, little of which has survived. Old manuscripts contain hints of this repertoire, such as the Triads which lists, in groups of three, characters and episodes from lore. The text alludes and mentions people and dramas of which we know nothing; thus, the Triads provide a tantalizing (and heartbreaking) glimpse of the breadth of the material lost. What does remain often defies neat, tidy, classical categorization. The gods appear as both divine and mortal, with their roles and charges shifting from sacred to mythological. The stories can and have been interpreted in different ways, and on occasion one is forced to rely on the common Celtic tradition from Irish or Breton legacies for guidance and help in piecing the Welsh remnants together.

In compiling the material for this deck, I chose to keep close to my source so as to remain faithful to the medieval Welsh material. Therefore, with its contradictions, gaps, and a medieval worldview that often resists whitewashing its heroes or heroines, the stories may seem unorthodox and unruly to the modern sensibility. These old tales present characters with a complexity of both honourable aspirations and shameful failings, such as the hero Pwyll, lord of Dyfed, who ruled well and was much loved by his people, yet allows bullying in the form of the "Badger in the Bag" game, much to the disgust of his father-in-law. The magician Gwydion is another who illustrates this dual nature in trickery, trying to help ease his brother's suffering but then resorting to deception and misuse of his powers in bringing about the death of Pryderi. In an effort to preserve the integrity of the Welsh material, I have limited speculation or interjections that may compromise either tradition for the sake of conformity. While the mythology and the tarot may be of disparate traditions, the common threads of archetypal characters and dramas that run through both make for a cross-fertilization and a compatible marriage.

Wales has a treasure in its early verse manuscripts that is known as the Four Ancient Books of Wales, the titles of which alone create an air of respect and make one want to stand on ceremony: they are the Black Book of Carmarthen, the Book of Aneirin, the Book of Taliesin, and the Red Book of Hergest. The books were likely compiled in the thirteenth century but are copies of far older writings. The age and obscurity of some of the language forced even its medieval transcribers to question its meaning. Much material termed "traditional" derives from these books, such as the aforementioned Triads, the Stanza of the Graves, and the *Mabinogion*.

The famous collection of tales known as the *Mabinogion* are translated mostly from the Red Book and renamed by Lady Charlotte Guest. The word *mabinogion* is actually a ghost word, deriving from *mabinogi*, which can be loosely translated to mean "tales of a hero's boyhood." The main source for the myths and romances of this deck is the *Mabinogion*. The material is thought to have been composed between 1225 to 1425 but is likely derived from older material, especially in the case of the Four Branches. The collection contains twelve tales, with the Four Branches considered the most important in preserving great mythic figures such as Pwyll, Branwen, Manawydan, and Math. The stories are a lively brew, fused together and retold by a talented but unknown author who is thought to have been from the land of Dyfed in the south of Wales. Whoever he was, he loved his subject, and the *Mabinogion* is a rich, evocative world inhabited by vivid, personable characters.

The writings of Geoffrey of Monmouth have also been intrinsic in creating this deck, for he is a preserver of Myrddin and creator of the popular Merlin. His work also incorporates some of the traditional Welsh material that would otherwise be lost by way of oral tradition. His twelfth-century book *Historia Regum Britanniae*, "History of the Kings of Britain," retold and recharged the Arthurian legend amongst other heroic chapters. It was a very popular work in his day, with numerous copies having survived. It is thought his subsequent work, *Vita Merlini*, "Life of Merlin," was meant for a smaller audience and is a long poem inspired in part by the historical Myrddin, a bard who, according to the Welsh, went mad in a battle in 575, then retreated to the wilderness.

While the bibliography supplies a list of the many titles that have been valuable in compiling the material for this deck, special mention should be made of *The Welsh Fairy Book*—a much loved and cited classic now conveniently back in print.

Lastly, there is the matter of King Arthur, as Wales is steeped in Arthurian tradition. While the king and his knights do make appearances in this deck, the stage has purposely been given over to allow the country's lesser-known legends to shine. In my early twenties, I created *Legend: The Arthurian Tarot*, which was my first work and one that remains close to my heart, for it gave me the opportunity to resurrect some old Arthurian tales, sights, and passages rarely visited by the mainstream. These lesser-known stories are no less worthy; rather, their neglect is a result of there being so many beautiful facets to the medieval world that some are simply forgotten along the way.

This deck, having the title of Llewellyn—as the Welsh namesake of its publisher—provided the opportunity to serve the Welsh mythology in the same way *Legend* did the Arthurian, and thus presented the special circumstances needed for me to agree to create a second tarot deck. The medieval world of the Welsh, particularly in the *Mabinogion*, is very real, tactile, even rustic, with an Otherworld that overlaps and infringes on reality's borders. Poetic but rarely sentimental, the mortals anticipate and brace themselves for testing encounters with the Otherworld's shadow. To live within the reach of the supernatural is seen as natural, and sometimes a blessing and sometimes a hazard. This mystic realism is, I feel, one of early Celtic literature's most appealing qualities. It is not fantasy but organic reality, seen on occasion through an imaginative lens—in the same manner and beauty as the artistic tradition of the tarot.

The Noble Tarot

The tarot is an old, sophisticated set of images that was not used for fortunetelling until the eighteenth century. None can be certain of its origins, but the earliest decks to survive date from the mid-fifteenth century as a detail of Italian courtly life and a fine example of Renaissance art. The tarot deck is divided into what are called the trump cards or major arcana (*arcana* meaning "secrets") and minor arcana. The twenty-two major arcana images are detailed allegorical figures, concepts, virtues, or events. The minor arcana number fifty-six and divide into court cards and four suits, which are simple designs depicting the symbol of the suit in the number of the card, such as two swords illustrating the Two of Swords. Given the magical, religious, and mythological nature of the trumps, it is thought that they were originally a path of knowledge meant for meditation, or perhaps a device for teaching or storytelling, having many of the same archetypal players seen on the theatrical stage of the time. It could be, too, that they were a special treasure simply to be appreciated over long hours both for the art and for the higher truths they symbolized. The cards were certainly a status symbol, for few could afford the original art. The Visconti-Sforza deck is the best known and most complete of these early decks and is available in reprints. It is not known when the minor arcana cards were married to the trumps, but they are thought to be of Arab origin, passing by way of Moorish Spain, and they were popular for gaming. Our modern playing cards are a child of the tarot, with the minor arcana making up the deck and the Fool card or Joker being the one trump card to make the transition. In the sixteenth century, the game of tarocchi became popular in parts of Europe, and with the distribution of the cards gambling became a problem—hence the church's objection to the tarot. In the late eighteenth century, the gypsies began to use the cards for fortunetelling, with great success. For all the time that has passed, these elegant, mysterious cards are alive and well, given the gypsy foresight to diversify their use. The tarot is appreciated for numerous reasons by a diverse audience who may have no interest in the fortunetelling aspect but appreciate the sophistication of the deck, such as art collectors, historians, philosophers, and laypeople. In my own case, it was the art that first attracted me and ignited an interest in the concepts contained in the cards—yet I have a respect for the fortunetelling aspect and delight in seeing the cards laid out by Chance! And there is no denying that the modern-day health of the tarot is due to it being so well suited to the divining arts.

The Language
and Nature
of the Cards

The imagery of the traditional tarot deck has stayed much the same since the Middle Ages. *The Llewellyn Tarot* draws largely upon the art of the early Visconti tarots for the trump cards, and loosely on the popular Rider-Waite designs for the minor arcana. Though each artist envisions according to personal style, the image is kept within bounds of tradition. This is a traditional deck in retaining the age-old imagery and standard card interpretations, but it has the added aspect of being seen through the lens of medieval Wales in setting, character, and mythology. The tarot title of the card sits below the painting, while the Welsh title appears above. There may be, on rare occasion, a Welsh substitute in image, such as the Strength card depicting a man overcoming a wild boar rather than the lion customary to the card. Nearly if not all the time, counterparts in the tarot and Welsh tradition can be found, but it is not always seamless; the Universe card is a rare instance where the traditional tarot element of the female figure of Liberty dancing has been incorporated into the scene of Cadair Idris. She appears formed by the flurries of snow that dance about the summit and thus does not disrupt or overwhelm the scene, which normally would not contain a woman. The tales paired to each card help to reinforce and bring depth and context to its traditional meaning by way of a story or character's example. In some cases, the card will illustrate a scene from a story that began, or will unfold, in a direction beyond and unrelated to the meaning assigned to the card; in such instances it is the moment depicted in the scene of the card that is the intended focus of a reading, and not the proceeding or latter fate. For example, Branwen appears in a time of hope in the Star card, but her later life is not to be envied or applied, for she has one of the sad tales of Welsh mythology.

In bearing the Welsh name of Llewellyn, this deck appropriately celebrates the roots of its publisher in illustrating Welsh mythology. Llew was a multitalented god of light, a solar deity with his name meaning "bright" or "fair." For more on the founder and history of Llewellyn Publications, see the foreword by president Carl Llewellyn Weschcke, who helped make it the famed publishing house that it is today.

The major arcana cards illustrate archetypal characters, events, and passages in life. They may represent a mental or emotional state of being, or an aspiration. Like mythology, the tarot is a creative expression of the internal experience of life and the forces of nature—in essence, an externalized drama of development. Both can be seen as a map or path concerning the deeper questions of life, and both use the language of symbol. The cup, for example, speaks universally of nourishment. The major arcana have been termed gatekeepers of higher knowledge, and they may be thought of as the hand of destiny in one's life or as potent cards of fate meant to initiate growth. The minor arcana represent lesser details—mundane and mortal, they are a supporting cast of influences, like leaves to the rose, that are factors within one's control. For this reason, a minor arcana painting is also minor art in comparison with the trumps; like a single acoustic guitar contrasted with a symphony. The minor arcana of this deck follow the well-known scenes of the Rider-Waite cards and yet contain some of my imaginative details and are not a slave to the designs. The Rider-Waite images, which were drawn by Pamela Colman Smith in the early nineteen hundreds, are familiar to many, having become a standard in modern times, which was a favouring factor when conceiving this deck, which is intended to be accessible to beginners.

Intuition and the Cards

Not all who read the tarot claim any special psychic ability. Those aligned with their intuitive sense will find it easier to cultivate a rapport with the cards, just as some are more inclined to be musical. But much good can come of a straightforward traditional reading that is to be done directly via the standard interpretations listed in this book and the powers of deduction. Oftentimes the benefits of a card reading lie in sparking creative thinking and a new perspective applied to a situation or a querent's life in general. The configuration of cards can guide and resurrect one's life in helping to break an outmoded pattern of thought, present new possibilities, instill confidence, and encourage one to question priorities and future courses of action. In this respect, one need not believe in fate or any prophetic ability to benefit from the communion and focus that a card reading entails.

On first glance of a card layout, one ought to take note of any intuitive impressions that may arise, such as "a feel for the way the wind is blowing." The tarot is read effectively with a combination of standard card interpretations and any intuitive insights that may arise and override the traditional meanings. A strong personal feel or impression as to the meaning of the card on any particular day is given more weight than the traditional interpretations. Readers are encouraged to follow their instincts in this regard. Visual art has the power to speak a thousand words, and the traditional imagery of the tarot is especially evocative and designed to stimulate the intuitive sense. The major arcana is the realm of visionary art, in that it depicts the otherwise unseen forces, virtues, and states. Hence, the importance of soulful art to the workings of the tarot. The intuition may be communicated by a "feel"—say, for example, hot or cold, a spontaneous impression, a word, idea, or even a visual flash in the mind's eye of a symbol, scene, or person. Not every reading will hold insights of the intuitive nature (or be interpreted correctly), but the conducive atmosphere of a quiet, private setting and goodwill between the reader and querent will lend itself to a greater depth.

Paying attention to one's dreams and inner dialogue in general can help strengthen the intuitive sense. Why some people can see possibilities in the cards and others struggle cannot be explained other than individual inclination. Some can hear a potential arrangement to enhance an existing piece of music; others only hear what reaches their ears. While creativity, I suspect, is akin, it is still not the same as the sixth sense. My own approach to the cards is similar to painting with watercolour, in that I watch the way the paint settles in the tooth or grain of the paper for possibilities to draw upon and tease out the pattern forming of its own accord. For example, the ferns that grow from the upper sleeves of the dress worn by the Priestess were formed in this manner, on their own—the leap lay in recognizing the faint potential and gently coaxing it into focus. It is a delicate process, as with reading the cards; one does not want to preempt or stubbornly impose a preconceived idea. Yet, with painting, the artist is free to infuse personality, whereas with a card reading the less involved or removed the reader remains, the better. A factor that can seriously hinder a card reading is the emotional attachment of the reader to the outcome. Vigilance is required to keep bias at bay, particularly when reading for one's self.

Some Misconceptions

The tarot has suffered some misconceptions in the past, which fortunately seem to be lessening as more people study the cards. At one time, film enjoyed sensationalizing the deck, but now uses it more often as a poetic device. It is not the "wicked pack" as some once preached. Nor does it have any particular religious affiliation, being that its imagery and concepts cross ethnic, cultural, philosophical, and religious boundaries. The tarot can be a powerful tool and unfortunately there are those who have used it to manipulate others and situations to their own advantage. More often good comes of the tarot, but as a card reader one must be continually aware and sensitive as to what information is relayed and in what manner. All must be tempered with common sense. Sometimes being responsible may mean gently refusing to read for someone you deem overly impressionable or susceptible. Overuse can also be a problem, in taxing the energy of the reader or developing an unhealthy dependence on the cards.

The Reversed Card

Though fewer readers employ reversed interpretations of the cards, they appear in this book out of respect for the reader's right to choose. I do not, however, advocate the use of reversed interpretations, believing the tarot to be a balanced system of positive and negative influences without turning cards upside down. Reversed cards are by their nature abhorrations, lacking the full-bodied message of the upright position and generally making for an unnecessarily vague, gloomy, disjointed reading.

The Layout of the Cards

Before attempting to read the cards, one is advised to spend some time becoming familiar with the images, noting any personal impressions of the cards before learning their traditional interpretations. This personal connection with the deck is an important element that will enhance your readings.

Before shuffling the cards, some readers like to choose a card called the significator, which they deem best describes the querent or situation being questioned. The significator is the first card to be placed on the table and is thought to aid focus and anchor the card reading.

The reader or the querent may shuffle the cards, and then the querent ought to cut the deck once. The reader then draws ten cards and places them faceup in the order and position noted by the diagram, which in this case is the classical layout known as the Celtic Cross, followed by the Horseshoe spread, which is popular for concise, quick readings.

Next, take an overview of the cards. Note the number of trump cards compared with the minor arcana as a clue to the weight of the reading. Also take into account any predominant suit, since they will give a sense of whether the reading is based on actions, as in swords; the intellect, as in wands; the heart, as in cups; or the material world, as in pentacles. It is important also to see the card within the context of its neighbouring cards, which can strengthen or weaken its significance.

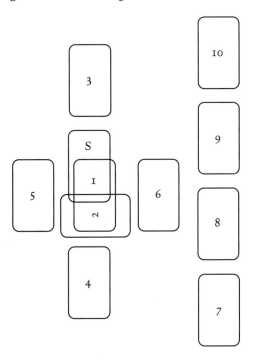

The Celtic Cross Spread

The Celtic Cross Spread: Interpretation of Card Positions

Significator: The card chosen to represent the querent or situation being questioned.

Position 1: Indicates the querent in relationship to the present situation.

Position 2: Represents the positive forces or assets in the querent's favour. If this card should happen to be a negative card, it indicates the nature of an obstacle that is hindering progress. (The card in this position is always interpreted in its upright manner.)

Position 3: Can be viewed as a message from the higher self. It can also reflect the querent's potentials and aspirations.

Position 4: Represents the preoccupation of the subconscious, which filters into waking life, affecting moods and outlook. This is the underlying theme of dreams and the emotional undercurrent in the querent's life.

Position 5: Represents past events and influences that colour and give rise to the current situation.

Position 6: Represents the state of the querent's relationships with others.

Position 7: Indicates the querent's psychological state and attributes that can greatly affect the outcome of the matter.

Position 8: Represents the querent's environment and unseen forces influencing the situation.

Position 9: Indicates the hopes and fears of the querent.

Position 10: Indicates the outcome of the matter.

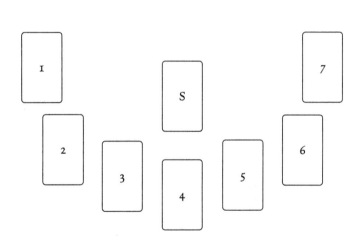

The Horseshoe Spread

The Horseshoe Spread:
Interpretation of Card Positions

Significator: The card chosen to represent the querent.

Position 1: Past conditions.

Position 2: Querent's present situation.

Position 3: Future outlook.

Position 4: Best approach to the situation.

Position 5: The attributes of others surrounding the querent.

Position 6: Challenges to be faced.

Position 7: The final outcome.

The ·Major· Arcana

0: The Fool

DESCRIPTION

The traditional tarot imagery depicts a man on the verge of stepping off a ledge. The Fool is usually dressed in warm colours, sometimes a jester's costume or the plain clothes of a traveler, and carries a stick or bundle over his shoulder. A white dog is the Fool's traditional travelling companion and is sometimes seen to be nipping at his heels.

Peredur

Peredur was the seventh son of Evrawc, and in Welsh tradition the original hero of the Grail quest. Some will recognize the character as Percivale (Parsi-fal = "pure fool"), a knight of the Round Table in the Arthurian legend. In the Mabinogion, we are given an early view of the character and a raw version of the Grail quest. Peredur appears as a more organic knight, and while the quest is rich with mysteries surrounding the Grail, it is driven by the archaic motif to avenge the death of a cousin whose head lies on a platter. Peredur's journey from fool to exalted hero and Grail guardian is long, imaginative, and humorous, with many adventures. It is also made sublime with otherworldly passages that form the Grail tradition. Here, we join him for his early fool days…

Peredur grew up without his six brothers and father, all of whom had all died in dangerous knightly pursuits. His mother, thinking to save him from the same fate, raised Peredur in a remote part of Wales, far from the lure of knighthood. His company was restricted to spiritless men and women, and he spent much of his time wandering the woods throwing sticks and staves—a pastime that well served the future knight. He was athletic, with speed enough to herd hinds, which he once drove home to his mother thinking them goats who had lost their horns in the wild. Young Peredur suffered an arrested development in his sheltered upbringing. He was thrilled to see a small band of knights travel through the woods one day, and when he asked his mother what sort of creatures they were, she told him they were angels. However, Peredur later caught up to the riders and plagued Owaine with unending questions as to the nature of a knight. With his imagination fired and heart set, Peredur confronted his mother with her lie and announced his plan to leave home for the life of arms. In the face of her worst fears, his mother swooned.

Having chosen the strongest pony, Peredur set about making reins and trappings from twigs, and pressed a pack into a saddle, all in the fashion of the knight's accoutrement. Seeing that he could not be deterred, his mother advised him to seek out King Arthur to be made a knight, explaining that his followers were the best of men. She also advised him to attend church, eat well, aid distressed women, possess and then be generous with jewels, and seek the love of a fair, esteemed woman, as she would reflect well on him. With nothing but a handful of sharpened sticks, Peredur mounted his piebald pony and rode forth into the wilderness. He traveled days through the deserted landscape until coming upon a tent, which he assumed to be a church. On entering, he found a woman who wore a large ring, and at her side stood a table set with food. Peredur told her of his mother's advice to eat well, and his hostess obliged. After his fill, he bent down on one knee before the maid and told her of his mother's advice concerning jewels, at which she gave him her ring and he departed. The woman told her returning lover of the extraordinary events. He was a suspicious, cruel man and dragged her off in a long search for the fool. (Much later she would be rescued and redeemed by Peredur.)

Meanwhile, at Arthur's court, a knight tried to provoke a fight by throwing liquor in the face of the queen and making off with a golden cup. He then camped in the meadow below the castle, awaiting a knight to champion the queen and avenge the insult. As the court pondered the challenge, Peredur entered the hall on his pony. To the dismay of onlookers, he rode the length of the room and announced to Kai, Arthur's seneschal, that he had come for his knighthood. Kai then led the court in making fun of the fool, at which time two dwarfs objected, referring to Peredur as "chief of warriors," foreshadowing his supremacy in arms. This only served to fuel Kai's anger, who then sent the innocent fool out to challenge the knight in the meadow, whom all others feared to fight. The knight strutted up and down the field, impressed with his own strength, and when insulted at the assumptions of the boy, gave him a forceful shot between the shoulders with the shaft of his spear. Peredur recovered and threw one of his forked sticks, which inflicted a serious head wound and brought a swift death. Fearing harm might come to the young fool, Owaine left his fellow knights in the hall to find Peredur dragging the body of the dead knight about the field. On asking what he was doing, Peredur replied that he was trying to take the iron coat from the body. Owaine then introduced the fool to the workings of buckles and helped him don his newly acquired armour. Peredur explained that he had no intention of returning to the court whilst Kai was there, and he pledged to avenge the abuse of dwarfs in the future. He then gave the goblet to Owaine and mounted the dead knight's horse to ride off into the wide world to "earn his stripes" or "spurs," as would be the mark of a medieval knight.

Peredur later becomes one of the best knights to sit at the Round Table. The path ahead leads him to the Fisher King, lessons with his Grail-guarding uncles, and failure. Love and battles await, as well as testings of sovereignty and many wonders—such as sheep of ever-changing colour, a miraculous burning tree, and a chess board with pieces that come to life and play of their own accord. After his early failure in the presence of the Grail, Peredur searches most of his life to find the Grail castle a second time, and with it comes redemption.

UPRIGHT

A beginning. Embarking. Establishing a path. A leap of faith. Venturing off on one's own. New possibilities. Optimism. Not being limited by previous experience or the opinions of others. An open mind. A break with convention. Nonconformity. Lack of reason. Deliberate ignorance. Folly. Learning through play. Testing and exploring. Acting without a plan. Being open to new experiences. Enthusiasm. Trust. Innocence. Choosing a path that may appear foolish to others. Unrealistic expectations. Being in the present. Uninhibited behaviour. Chasing rainbows. Being blissfully unaware of dangers allows one to reach a higher goal. Or, if aware of the danger, choosing not to let fear hold one back.

REVERSED

Missed opportunity. Having the attitude of a spoiled child. Arrested development. Crippling insecurity as a result of a sheltered life. Poor work ethic. Lack of conviction, purpose, or avoiding responsibilities by aimless wandering. Unfulfilling travels. Inability to recognize opportunities, or not being willing to work for them. Failure to learn. Cowardice. Lack of humour.

I: The Magician

DESCRIPTION

In the traditional tarot imagery, the magician stands with one arm raised over a table, upon which lie the symbols of the minor arcana suits—sword, cup, and disk, while the (hazel) wand of the magician is held in hand, representing his command over these aspects of life and suggesting he is a conduit of unseen powers. The figure eight symbol associated with the card appears in the pattern of his cloak, representing the infinite circling of the polarized energies of nature.

Gwydion

Gwydion was the gifted nephew of Math, lord of Gwynedd, the beautiful and rugged land of north Wales. He was said to be unrivaled as a storyteller in a country that teemed with talent. Like his uncle, he also had the gift of magic, and his name reflects this nature with Gwydion meaning "scientist magician." The characters of Math and Gwydion naturally bring to mind the subject of the druids, reminding us of the importance of the isle of Anglesey as a druidic centre for Europe. Sadly this small book can only give a brief note to the rich druidic history and related sites to be found in Wales, and encourage the titles noted in the bibliography as respected works on the subject. In the mythology of Wales, Gwydion is an active magician, appearing in the cryptic and powerful poem Cad Goddeu, "Battle of Trees," where various types of trees become an animated fighting force to meet in an awesome battle. In the Mabinogion he is seen as the caring guardian of Llew Llaw Gyffes (see the Wheel of Fortune and Sun cards). However, the fourth branch of the Mabinogion begins with a tale where we see the ambivilant nature and dangers of the young magician.

Math, son of Mathonwy, lord of Gwynedd, had an imaginative requirement to life in that his feet had to rest in the lap of a virgin or he would cease to exist. The only time he could walk the land was when his country was at war and in need of him. Gwydion had a brother, Gilfaethwy, who suffered a great passion for Math's virgin foot-holder, and yet with Math ever present and his ability to hear all whispers if caught by the wind, Gilfaethwy was prevented from wooing the girl. As his brother weakened with lovesickness, Gwydion devised a plan and convinced Math to send him and his brother on a mission to win the magical swine that belonged to Pryderi, ruler of Dyfed in the south. Gwydion told Math of the small beasts that had been given to Pryderi by his friend Arawn, the lord of the Otherworld. He explained that the creatures were called pigs by some and swine by others, and that their meat would be better than oxen. Gwydion, Gilfaethwy, and a company of ten men posed as bards and were well received by Pryderi. As "chief of song," Gwydion sat beside Pryderi and recited tales to enthrall the court, who agreed he was the finest storyteller in the land. His host was most appreciative and offered the bard his choice of reward. Yet Pryderi could not be persuaded to part with his pigs, explaining that he was bound by a covenant to the land which would not allow any gifting of the animals until they had reproduced and doubled their numbers. Gwydion noted that an exchange was not forbidden by the covenant and the following day he conjured twelve gilded shields from fungus, twelve magnificent horses with saddles of gold, and twelve black greyhounds with white breasts and collars of gold, and then proposed an exchange of animals. Pryderi accepted, but once the bards and swine were on their way north, the illusion of horses and hounds began to dissolve and vanished into the air. Realizing he had been tricked, Pryderi gave chase and events escalated to a state of war, at which time Math joined the battlefront. It was agreed that Pryderi and Gwydion alone should decide the battle in man-to-man combat. And by Gwydion's hand and magic, Pryderi met his death. Math later returned home to find Gilfaethwy had raped Goewin, the virgin foot-holder, in his absence. With the trickery surrounding the death of Pryderi and the rape of Goewin, the nephews were now fugitives, to whom none would give shelter. Math devised a punishment for the two and with a touch of his wand changed them into the shape of a stag and hind to live in the wilderness for the period of one year. The second year they returned to Math, who then placed them in the shapes of a boar and sow, taking care to reverse their genders. In the third year they were forced to live and learn as a pair of wolves, and then, with time served, Math restored them to their own skins to live on as rehabilitated men.

UPRIGHT

Talent and intelligence. A higher-comprehending mind. Purpose and skill. Independent thinker. Self-rule. Freedom. A person who is a force of art and creativity. Intuition. An inspiring, powerful voice. Commitment and communication. Eloquence and persuasion. Charm, confidence, and control. Talent that carries responsibility and casts one in an otherworldly light. Leadership and influence. Showmanship and dexterity. An ambiguous card, as the magician is also a trickster, a shadowy ringmaster, and a juggler. The unevolved magician character is a creature of appetite, impulse, and manipulation. Disregard of others and self-aggrandizing behaviour (resembling the rock star gone awry).

REVERSED

Deception. Gimmicks and tricks substituting for art. A showoff and profiteer. Unscrupulous liar and cheat. The hijacking of an art for personal gain. A superiority complex. The borrowed robes of an imposter. Shapeshifter. Falsehood.

2: The Priestess

DESCRIPTION

The traditional tarot imagery depicts a woman usually seated between a light and a dark pillar (in this case, light and shadow), representing the dual energies of nature. She wears fine robes and holds a book or other symbol of wisdom or talent in her lap. Sometimes a crescent moon rests at her feet or appears as a cornet or crown upon her head. She is often veiled or wears a wimple to represent being somewhat removed from ordinary life.

Ceridwen

Ceridwen has been styled "goddess of the witches" by the nineteenth-century influential Welsh folklorist Elias Owen. She can be seen as an early, powerful goddess bestowing artistic grace from her cauldron of inspiration and knowledge. In early poetry her cauldron is named as the source of "sweet awen," awen meaning "inspiration" or "muse." Ceridwen may also appear as an enchantress, crone, or a fierce and lively witch. Even in her folkloric guise the former goddess retains her formidable power. The name Ceridwen means "fair and beloved," yet it has been argued that the original form of the name is Cyrridfen, which in turn leads back to the root meaning of "hooked, crooked" woman. It seems she could be both the fair maid and crone, much like the goddesses who personify the land (also see the Justice card), reflecting her different moods, seasons, and conditions. Thus, the painting of this deck shows her to be formed out of the landscape, having a dual nature in one side of her body being in light, youth, and spring, while the other side lies in shadow, age, and winter. Two of Ceridwen's children also mirror the two polarities, with light and beauty in her daughter Creirwy, and the dark and ugly in her son Afagddu. The tale known as "Hanes Taliesin" preserves Ceridwen in folklore and is thought to be of ninth-century origin, though the earliest manuscript to survive dates from the sixteenth century. It is a popular, entertaining tale concerning the boy named Gwion Bach, who serves the witch Ceridwen in tending her cauldron of inspiration, before his second life as the great poet Taliesin…

On an island in the middle of Bala Lake lived Tegid Foel and his wife, Ceridwen. They had a son named Morfan ("great crow"), whom none would engage at the battle of Camlann as he looked like the devil. They also had a beautiful daughter named Creirwy ("dear one"), and lastly a son named Afagddu, who was so ugly that his mother feared he would not find any comfort or place in society without any redeeming qualities, and so she set about brewing a cauldron of poetic inspiration and knowledge for him. She charged a boy named Gwion Bach to stir the cauldron and a blind man named Morda to kindle the fire while she collected herbs and raised power to imbue the mixture. It was a complex task and required the brew to simmer for a year and a day. By accident, three drops splashed upon Gwion's fingers, which he quickly put in his mouth to cool, whereby he became the recipient of the gift of inspiration and knowledge. Immediately he understood the gravity of his situation and the awesome power of Ceridwen. With the foresight of her anger, he fled. The cauldron broke in two, leaving the remaining liquid to poison the waters of a stream and then the horses of Gwyddno. Ceridwen was outraged at the loss and struck Morda, then went after the boy. On seeing her approach, Gwion changed himself into a hare and picked up speed, but she then shifted her shape into a greyhound. He ran for the river and became a fish; she in turn gave chase as an otter. He took to the air as a bird, and she followed as a hawk. Just as her shadow overcame him, he spied a heap of wheat and became a grain. Ceridwen landed as a black hen and ate him. Nine months later she gave birth to Gwion, but could not bring herself to kill the child and so wrapped him in a leather bag and cast him out to sea.

The babe was eventually found in a weir by the young man Elphin. The weir was known to give up great quantities of fish every May eve, and while Elphin's father thought him a hapless, unlucky burden upon the family, he had decided to give the boy one chance at a future by tending the weir May eve. But no fish were to be found, only the leather. Elphin stayed calm in the face of the men who cursed his presence as the cause. Elphin remarked that there may yet be value in the weir, and made way to rescue the bag. On seeing the child, he exclaimed, "Behold a radiant brow!"—whereby the bard came by his name Taliesin, meaning "radiant brow." With care and tenderness, Elphin carried the babe home, and all the while tears ran down his cheeks in lament of his lost chance and fear of his father's disgust. Though in the body of a babe, Taliesin was still the gifted bard. He was moved to speak, and encouraged Elphin with a poem that foretold his prosperous future. The young man was amazed and asked the child if he was man or spirit. Later that night, Elphin's father, in contrast, felt the lash of the bard's tongue as Taliesin cut short his abuse of Elphin, stating that the lad had, in saving him, ensured more fortune in one night than the weir had brought the father in an entire lifetime. And so began Taliesin's childhood in the warm household of Elphin, to be followed by a life of poetic genius. (Also see the Hierophant card for the historical Taliesin.)

UPRIGHT

Faith and inspiration. Wisdom and insight. Enlightenment. Imagination. Receptive state of mind. Intellectual growth. Leading a life close to inspirational sources. Conducive, artistic environment. A rich inner life. Seclusion. Self-knowledge. An understanding of dark and light nature. A multifaceted, complex woman. Multiple talents. Creativity. A fertile, artistic, or scientific mind that benefits from intuitive or psychic leaps. Revelation. Expanding mind. The feminine artistic, creative force. The grace of inspiration. Choosing to serve an art or science, which can appear cold to those who live for relationships or misguided to those who serve money. A counsellor, priestess, anchoress. A woman who appears removed emotionally and who is a law unto herself (this, however, does not mean she is unkind, and being impartial she often makes a wise counsellor). Self-reliance. The card may represent avoiding commitment to a relationship. While she may be an inspiring role model herself, she is not the sort to seek followers. A mature woman. A time of peace. Charging of energy. Insight and foresight. A keeper of inspiring sources, whether ideas, beauty, or life by example.

REVERSED

Withholding knowledge or sources. A manipulator or fraud. Superficial show of knowledge. One playing the role of haughty queen. Ignorance. Egoism. Waste of talent. Hollow existence. Jealousy.

3: The Empress

DESCRIPTION

The traditional tarot imagery depicts a woman comfortably seated in fine robes. Most often she is outside, surrounded by nature, symbolizing the fertility of the card. She holds a scepter and orb, symbols of the royal and the feminine. A shield rests at her feet, which is usually decorated with a design that harkens love or Venus, such as a heart or swans.

Rhiannon

Rhiannon, meaning "great queen," was the otherworldly wife of Pwyll, ruler of Dyfed. Like other characters of the Welsh tradition she is thought to have once been a goddess, but with time and an eroding Christian influence, she survives demoted to an otherworldly wife. Rhiannon is equated with the Romanized Gallic equine goddess Epona. In the Mabinogion, she makes her first appearance riding a magical white mare. Her son's birth shares a mysterious parallel connection with a colt, and lastly she herself suffers a punishment of having to carry people on her back, as if she were a beast of burden. Tradition does preserve the birds of Rhiannon, who are her companions and a relic of her divinity. It is said their song was so potent an enchantment that it would wake the dead and place the living in a dream. In the Mabinogion, the character of Rhiannon, who resembles more fairy than goddess, falls in love with a mortal, Pwyll—a man with otherworldly associations. His land of Dyfed was an area of Wales where the veil between this world and the next was curiously, treacherously thin. Pwyll had exchanged places with Arawn, King of Annwn (meaning "otherworld"), for one year. (Also see the Death card.) Pwyll did not seem to suffer from climate change with his experience and he remained friends with Arawn, who bestowed upon him the title "Head of Annwn." An alliance and exchange had already been established when Rhiannon chose to cross boundaries for a mortal husband…

Pwyll was holding court at the royal seat of Arberth, and in the evening he went to sit on a sacred mound of earth that legend said was a portal to the otherworld and where none could pass the night without vision or adventure. As Pwyll sat patiently surveying the land, a woman riding a white mare appeared on the highway. He called to his men to fetch her, and while she looked to be travelling a gentle pace, none could catch her. The next day the scene was repeated and a faster horse failed to reach her. Pwyll suspected some illusion at play and rode out after her himself, but when his speed brought him no closer he called out to the woman asking her to stop; which she did, remarking that it would have been better for his horses had he asked long ago. She drew back her veil and fixed her eyes upon him, and he thought their beauty and depth beyond compare. He asked the purpose of her journey and she explained she had come on her own errand to find him. Pwyll was most pleased. She introduced herself and went on to explain that her love for him had prevented her from marrying any other. But now her father in the Otherworld had promised her to a man named Gwawl against her will, and she would not marry him unless Pwyll rejected her. Pwyll assured Rhiannon that she was his choice of all women. They then made a secret pledge to meet again in one year at her father's palace. When the day came, Rhiannon had arranged a wedding feast and all would have been well if Pwyll, in a thoughtless moment, had not agreed to grant an unconditional boon to a guest, who—unbeknownst to Pwyll—was the jilted suitor, who naturally asked for the bride.

A clever woman, Rhiannon was quick to stall the wedding yet another year and gave Pwyll detailed instructions to return on the date dressed as a beggar with a magic bag she gave him. As a beggar he could ask Gwawl for the bag's fill of food from the feast and, when the bag would not take its fill, Pwyll was to tell Gwawl that only a man of noble blood could quell the appetite by placing his feet in the bag. All unfolded as planned, and when the trusting Gwawl obliged, Pwyll quickly enveloped and trapped him in the bag. Pwyll's men then fell upon the hall and entertained themselves in beating the bag, calling their amusement "Badger in the Bag." An injured Gwawl protested that he did not deserve such treatment, and the disgusted father of the bride agreed. Pwyll called for a halt to the game, and then pressured Gwawl to return Rhiannon. Gwawl agreed and was released.

The couple returned to Dyfed, where Rhiannon became a kind and capable queen, but as she was foreign, the people were reluctant to accept her. Furthermore, as she had not given birth to an heir, Pwyll came under pressure to forsake her. He refused, and in the fourth year a child was born, but the babe was then mysteriously stolen from under the noses of six sleeping nurses. Thinking they would face the death penalty for their neglect, the nurses conspired to kill some puppies and smear the queen's hands and face with blood, accusing her of devouring her own child in the night. Rhiannon suspected the plot and promised the nurses protection for the truth, but they stood firm six to one. In the end, the queen herself asked for penance, rather than contending with the cruel company of the women. A council decided that for seven years she should sit each day at the horse block, where she would tell passersby of her crime and offer to carry them on her back to the castle.

Rhiannon's tale traveled to a friend of Pwyll named Teirnyon, who began to suspect the baby boy who had come into the keeping of him and his wife was the son of the lord of Dyfed. They took the child to court, and Teirnyon told the strange tale of how on the first of May a colt would be born to his mare, but would then mysteriously disappear. The same night of the Queen's alleged crime, he had stood guard over his mare and newborn foal to fight off the mysterious apparition of a black hand that had reached out of the dark to snatch the colt. In the wake of the unearthly creature, he had found the child, whom they then took in and raised as their own. All the court agreed the child was the image of Pwyll, his father. With the return of her son, Rhiannon named him Pryderi (meaning "care" or "anxiety"), and he grew up to be the capable, much-loved ruler of Dyfed. After the death of Pwyll, Rhiannon went on to marry the wise and respected Manawydan, son of Llyr. (Also see the Hanged Man card.)

UPRIGHT

A kind, capable woman. One who instills confidence in others. A beneficial influence. A strong role model. A woman who promotes and encourages the potential of those around her. A peacemaker and diplomat. An intelligent, calm, mature personality. Determination and dignity. One who teaches by example. A nurturing, considerate person who gives much to the community. Confidence. Empathy. A matriarch. Guidance and support. A mother figure. Security, comfort, and appreciation. Fertility. Personal development.

REVERSED

Doubts and hardship. Turmoil, extravagance. Lack of support or guidance. Cold comfort. Instability. Overly protective behaviour. Infertility or unplanned pregnancy.

4: The Emperor

DESCRIPTION

The traditional tarot imagery depicts a mature man comfortably seated upon a throne. He is draped in red for vibrancy and strength, and holds a scepter, symbol of male potency. The emperor is partially armoured to represent his readiness for battle, and the shield figures prominently, symbolizing his protective, defensive power.

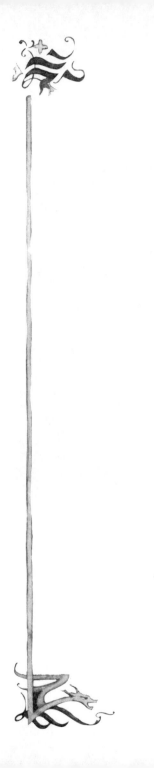

Bran the Blessed

Bran was the son of Llyr and brother to Branwen and Manawydan. Unlike his brother and sister who were of normal size, Bran was
colossal, able to wade across seas and housed by tents, as no building contained him. He was a forerunner of King Arthur, and some of his exploits
are echoed in the deeds of the Pendragons. Bran is also thought to have
provided inspiration for the figures of the Grail guardians in the Arthurian
world, who traditionally suffer an injury likened to Bran's wounded foot.
It seems people had long held Bran to be an exemplary model of kingship
and credited him as the source of the proverb "He who will be chief, let
him be a bridge"—referring to the responsibility and sacrifice of a king, to
whom more is given and from him more is required. Legend has it that
the country's enduring love for Bran led Arthur to feel pangs of jealousy,
and became his reason for disinterring Bran's head from its resting place
at White Mount London, where it had been buried as a talisman in protection of Britain. The name Bran means "raven," and the Tower of London is home to ravens today who have inherited the custom, for it is
believed their presence guards the island from invasion. (The modern
ravens are permanent residents of the Tower, having had their wings
clipped.)

The second branch of the *Mabinogion* tells of how Bran the
Blessed gave his sister Branwen to the Irish king
Matholwch in marriage. They had a son, Gwern, and all
was well until the foster brothers of the king

began to revisit old grievances, stoking their hatred of Branwen, making her suffer for the sins of her kinsman Efnisien (also see the Star card). Pressured by his family, Matholwch allowed shameful treatment of Branwen, but when word reached Bran, it was grounds for war. Raising an army, Bran marched on the Irish, who in their retreat destroyed a bridge over the river Llinon (Shannon). When faced with the current, Bran remarked, "There is no counsel except that he who will be chief, let him be a bridge." And so he lay across the river, allowing the host to pass over him. Under the looming threat of Bran and the Isle of the Mighty, the Irish repented the abuse of Branwen and in an effort to appease the Britons offered the crown of Ireland to Branwen's son Gwern, nephew to Bran. But Bran was not convinced. The Irish then built a huge hall capable of housing Bran, an honour the giant had not known before. But it was his desire for peace and his responsibility to avoid the devastations of war that finally brought Bran to meet the Irish under the same roof. Alas, the hall was a trap, and at the instigating of Bran's own half brother Efnisien (meaning "not peaceful"), the two sides fell into battle. It was a terrible, lengthy struggle, leaving, as legend has it, only five pregnant women alive to repopulate Ireland. Of the Britons, only seven men survived alongside Bran and his sister; with Manawydan and Pryderi among them. Bran had, however, suffered a poisoned wound to his foot. Knowing his death was near, he instructed his men to cut off his head, which he assured them would retain his spirit and live on to keep them company for years to come. The men did as Bran instructed, and the tale

takes on an otherworldly air as the men return to
Harlech with the head. For seven years the men
remained in the company of the head, which kept them
removed, as if under a spell, from the real world and its harsh
condition. After the seventh year, as per Bran's instruction,
they moved to the island of Gwales, off the southwest coast,
where they lived out the next eighty years. This period of time
has become known in legend as "the Entertaining of the
Noble Head." Their enchantment—a sort of between-
worlds—continued as the spirit of Bran lingered on and the
otherworldly birds of Rhiannon sang to them in their bliss.
Reality eventually reclaimed them when, just as Bran had
prophesized, one of the party opened a door which faced in
the direction of Cornwall, whereupon reality fell in upon
them, bringing waves of grief and breaking the spell. The
solemn company then carried out Bran's last wishes and took
the head to London, where they buried it at White Mount,
facing toward the continent, where it served as a talisman to
ward off invasion of Britain.

UPRIGHT

A strong leader. A man of power and responsibilities. Protection. Conviction and self-sacrifice. A strong, masculine influence. Integrity and ethics. A father figure. Worldly power. Stability and reason. Compassion. Wisdom and aid. Conquest. Masculine, sexual energy. A competitive nature. Fair play. Competence. A flexible mind open to the ideas of others. Established, relaxed authority. Courage. Reason ruling emotion. Thought for the greater good.

REVERSED

Irresponsible behaviour. Cowardice. Feeble efforts. Legal problems. Immaturity and ineptitude. Job loss. A miserable, short-tempered employer or father. Tyranny. Infertility. Impotence in life. Weakness. Injury.

5: The Hierophant

DESCRIPTION

The traditional tarot imagery depicts a mature man with a commanding presence seated between two pillars. He wears rich robes of office and in his left hand holds a symbol of the religious order to which he belongs. The card is sometimes titled the Pope, and in later versions includes two altar boys at his feet, over whom he traces a blessing.

Taliesin

The historical Taliesin was a bard with a powerful personality that can be felt through his poetry even at a distance of more than a thousand years. There are popular folktales surrounding Taliesin, which are retold with the Priestess card and therefore allow this segment to pursue the historical sixth-century character and his venerable profession. The Welsh bard with his poetic gift and power of influence may seem far removed from our modern time, but we can recognize the same talent, role, and responsibilities in the songwriters and musicians of today—the very best of whom may be termed bards, even if not officially inaugurated. A line of descent can be seen in the figure of Bob Dylan, who is rumoured to have taken the name "Dylan" in deference to the great modern Welsh poet Dylan Thomas. The writings of Dylan Thomas continue to influence lyrics today, and Thomas himself is a link in a remarkable long chain of Welsh poetry that reaches back to Taliesin.

The Welsh monk Nennius names Taliesin and four bards in his early medieval compilation *Historia Brittonum* as being the country's best, and Taliesin "chief of bards." Of those named, only the work of Taliesin and Aneirin survive, and as the earliest examples, they are considered the foundation stone of Welsh poetry. Aneirin "of flowing verse" is famed for the long poem Y *Gododdin*, a series of elegies for heroes fallen in battle. The Book of Taliesin, transcribed in the thirteenth century, contains numerous poems of varied subject and time, and of these, twelve poems are thought to be the authentic work of Taliesin.

The sixth century was a time of perpetual battle alert for the Britons (the native Celts of the island to include the Welsh), who were driven back by the invading Angles and Saxons. The Britons allied from Cornwall in the south, up along the west of the country, to the south of Scotland. This time is known as the Heroic Age, deep in battles, bravery, and blood, as Taliesin's poems attest. The bard is thought to have been a native of Powys, in northeast Wales, but his greatest poems stem from his time in the kingdom of Rheged, which now lies within the borders of northern England. His patrons were the heroic Urien, lord of Rheged, and his son Owaine (both of whom have been supplanted anachronistically in the Arthurian romances). The pagan court was an active, impressive resistance force, and as court bard, it was Taliesin's responsibility to make it the stuff of legend. Urien and Owaine are seen as generous, brave, and larger than life, leading one to question whether the shine comes from the singular talent of Taliesin or the mettle of the hero. The bard did, however, record less-flattering forays and had a reputation for daring honesty and ego, as seen in the later folklore, where as a boy he challenges the sycophantic bards of Maelgwn. All twelve surviving poems are in the Heroic tradition and powerful in praise of Urien as warrior—as Saunders Lewis translates, "To gaze upon him is widespread fear"; and then, referring to his leadership, "gold king of the Northland and of kings king" (Jarman, A *Guide to Welsh Literature*). By his own words, Taliesin did not take to the field himself but was witness to battle, and his poetry served as a weapon of (psychological) war in itself. He was the height and the standard to which bards aspired for a thousand years to follow.

Within the twelfth-century bardic hierarchy, *pencerdd* ("chief of song") was the highest-ranked bard, who would have held a special chair at court and been a bard of ceremony, one whose duties included singing the praises of God and his king. The lesser rank was the *bardd teulu* ("poet of the retinue"), whose responsibilities included entertaining the queen, and singing and rallying the warband before battle. The lowest rank would be the *cerddorion* (*joculators*, in Latin), serving the base appetite. A country that so valued its heritage and beauty of words naturally produced gifted lay poets and storytellers outside the profession, but the official bards' patience ran short with proud, lesser talents, whom they referred to as "vain," "petty," or "false bards." Before the demise of the druid, the intellectual class could be distinguished into three groups, with the druid being first; followed by the vates, a seer-poet; and the bard. It seems that, depending on the individual talent and personality, the lines of distinction and duties may overlap, as in the case of the figure of Myrddin (Merlin), who can be seen as all three. The druids were the elite intellectual class and to some extent presided over priestly and judicial functions of society. They were more powerful and less compromising, and thus made more enemies, than the vates or bards, who survived long after the druids' clash with Rome. The word *vates* was the name given to the poet/seer/philosophers of the ancient Celtic society in Gaul. The Welsh called their class of prophetic poets *awenyddion*, meaning "inspired people" (also see the Universe card). The Welsh word *awen* is used to describe inspiration or poetic muse and is related to the word *awel*, meaning "breeze," which together give the impression of "breath of the muse"—a worthy shard of poetic beauty itself. The *fili* ("one who sees") of Irish tradition is also comparable, whose special gift of visionary poetry was symbolized by a branch adorned with silver bells, reminiscent of the scented branch of the Otherworld. Welsh bards were said to mark branches of hazel with their poetry. They were the official minstrels and composers of verse. By some claims their memorized repertoire of myth was so vast as to require days for the telling. The bard was, by impact of his art, a political force, involved in the crowning of kings and the keeper of royal genealogies. The bard could be rewarded well, with Taliesin, for example, having been given lands, all manner of jewelry, horses, cloaks of purple, and more. While it seems a genuine friendship and admiration existed between Taliesin and Urien, his king, the bard in general was to be treated with caution, for while his praises could bring lasting legend, as in the case of Rheged, he could, likewise, bring about dishonour and ruin with searing satirical power.

UPRIGHT

Authority. An advocate of tradition. Society's structure and code. The establishment. Orthodox behaviour. Adhering to tradition. Religious authority. A keeper or guardian of knowledge. Initiation. Instruction. The expectations of the outside world. Education. Following an established path. Benefiting from the strength of a group or tradition. The comfort of one's roots. Guidance. Clemency. Religious or educational institutions. Ritual, ceremony, and performance. A wedding or public alliance. Religious or spiritual inclination. Morals and ideals. Mediator. Interpreter. Mentor. Official faith and custom. Accepting a hierarchy. Depending on surrounding cards, can represent repression and the challenging of a system or of conventional wisdom. A person with the power to advance, challenge, or wrong another.

REVERSED

Crippling conservatism. Mind control. Self-delusion and egotism. Inappropriate, haughty behaviour. Thwarting the aspirations of others for a reason of insecurity. Conforming to be accepted. Hiding behind or blaming a tradition. Intolerance. Loss of trust. Abuse. Hostility.

6: The Lovers

DESCRIPTION

The traditional tarot imagery depicts a man and woman beneath an angelic figure thought to be Gabriel, or a winged cupid with his arrow poised to shoot. Sometimes a tree and serpent appear in the scene, harkening to Adam and Eve in Paradise. In some cases three people are depicted: a man and two women, emphasizing a choice to be made.

The Dream of
Macsen Wledig

Amongst the romances contained in the Mabinogion *is the tale of Macsen Wledig, who falls in love with a woman he sees in a dream. His character is based on the historical Emperor Magnus Maximus (AD 383–8) who came to Britain near the year AD 368 and married a Celt named Elen or Helen.*

M acsen was the handsome and wise emperor of Rome. He had yet to marry and no particular woman had stirred his imagination until one afternoon when a dream came to him. Macsen and his party had broken the hunt to pass the afternoon heat beside a river. The dream began with the river beckoning him to find its source, leading him over mountains, plains, rivers, and bridges of whalebone until he reached the sea. There Macsen boarded a ship built of planks which alternated gold and silver. He crossed over seas and passed through passages of fantastic rock to arrive at a rugged and mountainous land. There, at the mouth of the river, stood a fair castle. The dream continued to unfold, taking Macsen into the hall, where sat two young men with auburn hair playing *gwyddbwyll*, or chess. Beside a pillar sat the impressive figure of a hoary-headed man with armlets of gold and a torque about his neck. The chieftain passed his time by carving chessmen. Macsen's eyes cast further into the shadows to see a beautiful woman sitting in a chair of ruddy gold. She was dressed in white and gold and wore a frontlet of rubies and pearls. The woman rose with grace and came to stand before him. Macsen let his arms slide around her neck and waist and together they sank into the chair. As they rested cheek to cheek, the clamour of the rising hunt intruded upon the scene and Macsen awoke a changed man. He was no longer present, his spirit gone from him for love of the maiden. His love was immediate and to the root of his being, leaving him a troubled man as they returned to Rome.

In the weeks that followed, Macsen withdrew from the household, rarely ate or drank, only wasted away and slept so that he might revisit his dream. In the real world that surrounded him there was no sign of the maid. Time passed and the people of Rome began to say disparaging things of their emperor, without pity or knowledge of the love that possessed him. Eventually Macsen confided in the sage council of Rome, who in their wisdom suggested he send three messengers to search distant lands for the maid. In this way he would have the hope that at any moment she may be found, and this hope would sustain him.

Three years passed and still no maid had been found. Sorrow overtook Macsen once more. The situation became dire and so a royal friend suggested he return to the hunting ground where the dream had first come to him. And so Macsen returned and found a spot on the riverbank like that of his dream. He then sent messengers forth in the path of the dream, following the river's source, venturing westward to see the landscapes unfold as foretold. On reaching the maid in her rugged land, they hailed her as "Empress of Rome," to which she thought them mocking her. Nor did she believe their tidings of Macsen's dream and his great love, replying that if it be true then he would come to her himself. And that he did, finding all to unfold as his dream foretold—the boys at chess, the king carving with his time, and the beauty and love between he and the maid. She became his empress and has become known as Elen, or Helen of the Hosts. Legend says that she and her family helped restore Macsen to Rome after his throne was seized in his absence. Helen was much loved and remembered today by use of her name—"Helen's Highway"—to refer to stretches of Roman roads said to have been built under her direction by her devoted subjects.

UPRIGHT

Union of opposites. The promise or potential for love and romance. Partnership. Attraction, chemistry, lust. Magnetism. Harmony. Play. Joy. Humour. Romantic interlude or amorous encounter. Restless imagination. The crystallizing, projecting process of "blind love." High hopes. Flare of desire. Friendship, admiration, and affection. Communion. Sharing. On a deeper level it can represent transformational power of love. Inspiring feats to attain or secure love. Being made brave by love. Conviction and commitment. The mystic bond of familiar spirits. Mutual understanding. Fusion and energy. A pact. Symptoms of love: anxiety, vulnerability, short attention span. Being made useless by love. Poetry, daydreams, music. Expanding experience. Loss of the rational. Gratitude. Can represent a choice between what is desired and what is acceptable. Assessment. If a decision is involved, indicates happy outcome after struggles.

REVERSED

Temptation. Infidelity. Sweet nothings. Unworthy suitor. Careless treatment of others. Division. Conflict. Longing and frustration. Wasting in waiting. Love thwarted by interference and jealousy.

7: The Chariot

DESCRIPTION

The traditional tarot imagery depicts a chariot driven by a capable, partly armoured warrior. Speed is often indicated, representing the pace of life, yet the driver has a firm grip on the reins and remains in control of the situation. The chariot is drawn by two fantastical beasts or horses—one light, the other dark in colour—symbolizing the two opposing poles or dichotomy within a person, within the environment, or the impact of an event. The horses are reconciled to pull in tandem, bringing speed and progress.

Manawydan

Manawydan, son of Llyr (Llyr meaning "sea"), was brother to Bran the Blessed and Branwen. By marrying the widowed Rhiannon, he became a patient stepfather to Pryderi, and he is one of the most admirable, evolved temperaments in Welsh mythology. Manawydan is seen as the seasoned warrior, skilled and capable, with the wisdom and patience to triumph over the slippery opponents of the Otherworld. He is unusually humble in a heroic society where boasting is the fashion, and his understanding and respect for women further sets him apart. We know he was a disinherited prince, but we do not know why, and while the surviving Welsh material makes no mention of him in the role of a sea god, it is the long-standing consensus that he is the Welsh equivalent to the Irish Manannan Mac Lir. Tradition names his self-propelled boat Wave Sweeper, and he was said to be a glorious sight driving his chariot across the waves, as if the sea were a plain of flowers. The sea god is also associated with the Isle of Man, as its first king and guardian. Even today a bank of sea mist is referred to as "Manannan's Veil" by islanders. While time (and, likely, censoring Christian scribes) have stripped Manawydan of his former divine glory, the character seen in the Mabinogion is still the far-seeing, honourable survivor, Manawydan "of profound council."

The third branch of the Mabinogion tells of how, after burying the head of Bran at White Mount, Manawydan lamented that unlike his companions he had no home awaiting his return. Pryderi invited his friend to return with him to his land of Dyfed, where Manawydan and Rhiannon (Pryderi's widowed mother) took a liking to each other and soon were wed, to the delight of all. The land prospered under their reign, and together with Pryderi and his wife Kicva, the four were a tight-knit family. One evening a powerful enchantment descended upon Dyfed, which, when the mist lifted, left the land deserted of all its domestic livestock and inhabitants but for the two couples. In the third year of isolation, Manawydan thought it best to take the family to Lloegyr (England). They set up shop and Manawydan taught Pryderi how to make saddles, then lent his artistic gifts to decorating them with gold and blue enamel—the secrets of which he had learned from a master. Their enterprise was so successful that local saddle makers plotted to slay the two. On receiving a warning, Pryderi was indignant, saying he thought they ought to kill the boors, but Manawydan cautioned that evil fame and prison would then be their lot. They moved to another town and encountered the same scenario, this time with enameled shields. Manawydan judged the shoemakers of the third town to be too meek to assault them and so set about teaching Pryderi the craft of a shoemaker, and then taught himself the secrets of gilding so as to finish the clasps with gold. The shoes were exquisite, and resentment and eviction soon followed. With money made, the four then returned to Dyfed and lived comfortably, until one day Pryderi chose to ignore Manawydan's warning and entered a castle that was of a dangerous otherworldly nature, and thus walked into a trap. Manawydan resisted the lure, knowing he would be no match for the otherworldly power and cunning which conjured the castle. But, on hearing the tale, Rhiannon was blind to the fault of her son and turned on Manawydan, calling him an evil companion. She then disappeared into the night, found Pryderi, and became trapped in the same manner. A peal of thunder resounded, and the castle vanished with mother and son.

In the coming days, Kicva became increasingly aware of being alone with Manawydan. As her loneliness grew, she began to dwell on all wild imaginings of his desiring her until she whipped herself into a despair, not caring if she lived or died. Manawydan guessed the reason for her behaviour and broached the subject to reassure her she had nothing to fear. In a calm and steady tone, he swore he had only ever felt friendship for her, and even if in the dawn of youth he would not betray her friendship or the trust of Pryderi in such a way. Manawydan went on to assure her that he would do all in his power to see her through their grief and woe. With relief, Kicva told him that this is how she had deemed his character, and with renewed courage she followed Manawydan as he adapted to and navigated their changing conditions of fortune. First they returned to Lloegyr, where he once again earned their money as a shoemaker. Thinking of their survival, he then brought enough wheat seed to sow three fields in Dyfed. This new enterprise naturally aroused the curiosity of the Otherworld, who could not help but trespass his fields, thus providing Manawydan with an opportunity to catch one of their own and play out an elaborate ruse with which he could secure the release of Rhiannon, Pryderi, and the spell that held the land of Dyfed. (Also see the Hanged Man card.)

UPRIGHT

Triumph. Victory parade. Success of a multifaceted endeavour. Leadership, competence, and maturity. Conquest. An evolved personality. Courage. Being centered and secure. Moral, ethical progress and conduct. A high-minded, honourable approach to life. Balance, integration. Harmony of opposite tensions. Equilibrium. Reconciling opposing forces or views. Uniting right and left brain functions. Control over inner conflicts. Harnessing wild energies. Life unfolding at an accelerated pace, yet maintaining direction. Finding one's stride. Enjoying the thrill and ride of life. Engaging an ambition or dream. Achievement. High energy. Promotion, honours, and reward. Overcoming opposition. May indicate a rescue, as in the arrival of the cavalry.

REVERSED

Breakdown of an enterprise due to scattered energies. Doubts undermine and erode commitment and morale. Not having the confidence of a team. Weakness. Impulsive, erratic behaviour. Immaturity. Loss of focus. The tail wagging the dog. Being led astray. Loose cannon. Danger to come of too much power and speed.

8: Strength

DESCRIPTION

The traditional tarot imagery depicts a man or woman overcoming the strength of a lion or other beast. Sometimes the scene is a show of force, as in a man with a raised club, or an exercise in taming the beast, illustrated by a woman opening or closing a lion's jaws. In this card, Twrch Trwyth the boar represents physical animal strength, and the story entails a test of will, wiles, courage, and endurance in the vying for the comb, razor, and scissors that lay between his ears.

Twrch Trwyth

In the Mabinogion's tale of Kilhwch and Olwen, the young Kilhwch is required to accomplish a dazzling array of heroic tasks, with the help of an equally vast cast of characters, in order to win the hand of Olwen, daughter of a giant. Olwen was a lovely girl who left white flowers to grow in the impression of her footsteps. She was also a lonely girl, for her giant father, Yspaddaden Penkawr, killed all suitors who approached, believing the prophecy that his life would end with the marriage of Olwen. Kilhwch, whose mother had died when he was a baby, was a gentle young cousin of King Arthur. His stepmother suggested he marry one of her daughters and when he, startled by the prospect, claimed he was too young to marry, she snapped back that he would never have a wife unless it be Olwen. Kilhwch asked Arthur for help and a large company was assembled for the cause. The giant was as dangerous, defiant, and disagreeable as ever, and he set a bewildering array of difficult tasks for Kilhwch to achieve in his quest for Olwen. The story unfolds in lengthy, grand adventure in the accomplishing of the tasks, which varied from the laughable to the mystic in the collecting of the (live) whiskers of a notorious outlaw with which to make a leash to the freeing of the divine Mabon, a god of youth, from his mysterious imprisonment. However, most of the tasks were but preparation for the action-packed, humorous, and dangerous challenge which lay in retrieving the razor, comb, and scissors that rested between the ears of the fierce wild boar named Twrch Trwyth...

Arthur, Kilhwch, and company chased all about Ireland for days on end without capturing even one of the seven members of Twrch Trwyth's family. With all exhausted, the king decided to send Gwrhyr, who knew all languages, to speak with the boar and ask if he would meet with Arthur. Gwrhyr had many talents and prudently chose to take the mission in the shape of a bird. Twrch Trwyth had once been a king who, for some ill deed, had been transformed into a boar, and his family with him. All agreed that he was an impressive sight, with silver bristles like wire that flashed when he ran through the forest and gleamed on the plain. Twrch Trwyth refused to meet with Arthur, complaining to Gwrhyr that he and his family had suffered enough without men coming to pick fights with them. Gwrhyr then explained that they only came for the comb, razor, and scissors which lay between his ears. The boar was shocked at the impertinence and swore over his dead body would they have "the precious things" that lay between his ears. Furthermore, he promised that on the following day he and his family would travel to Arthur's own country and do great mischief. And they did—running riot, tearing up the land, and leaving truly fantastic carnage in their wake. Kilhwch, Arthur, and posse gave chase, and there were standoffs and wild, unsuccessful attempts to wrangle the boar, which left a long casualty list reaching so far as to include the death of Arthur's architect. Yet the men would not give up and the country saw no end to the shouting, barking, and snorting. At long last a crew including Arthur, Manawydan, and Mabon caught up to Twrch Trwyth, driving him off track to plunge into the waters of the Severn. Mabon spurred on his horse and snatched the razor while one of his companions grabbed the scissors, but the comb remained with Twrch Trwyth, who regained ground and disappeared over the horizon, leaving the company to recover their maimed and drowning men. It is said that the Severn was mild compared with the battle in Cornwall that finally yielded the comb, after which the beaten Twrch Trwyth and his remaining family took to the sea, never to be seen again.

The band of heroes went on to complete their last task in obtaining the blood of the witch Orddu who, continuing in the grand fashion of the tale, "lived on the confines of hell." In truth, Orddu lived in a cave in north Wales, where she gave a good fight and where Arthur had to be reminded that it would be unseemly for a king to be seen squabbling with a hag; he joined the fray regardless. With the witch subdued, blood in hand, the band returned to claim Olwen. The giant could not deny them and was killed by one of the men to have his head displayed on a stake outside of the castle. Kilhwch and Olwen were then joined in a long and happy marriage.

UPRIGHT

Courage. The determination to overcome obstacles. Inner strength. Spiritual strength. Consistent effort. Conviction. Having the strength to persevere. Being able to withstand naysayers and judgments of others and not be deterred. Facing one's fears. Being true. Harnessing passions that threaten to overwhelm but may be tamed with compassion and the will to overcome. Faith. Vitality. Ability to endure failures, losses, and disappointment, and yet keep the faith. Tenacity. Energy and intelligence. Work. Activity. Integrity. Focus and discipline. Overcoming. Outlasting competition or conditions. Reason and passion unite to bring strength.

REVERSED

Cowardice. Breakdown. Not wanting to succeed and choosing surrender—which is sometimes wise. Brittle, unflexing, outmoded dogma saps strength. Doubts. Anger. Impulsive behaviour. Acting on appetite alone. Strong enemy. Unjustified use of strength. A bully.

9: The Hermit

DESCRIPTION

The traditional tarot imagery depicts an old man walking toward the left of the card with a staff in hand. He is dressed in long robes and is generally hooded. Sometimes he holds a lantern that lights his way and sheds enough light to see the surrounding wild, uninhabited landscape and the serpent of wisdom at his feet. In earlier decks he holds an hourglass rather than a lantern, and he is a figure thought to have evolved from (Father) Time or Saturn.

Myrddin

The popular image of Merlin as magician and prophet is largely the creation of Geoffrey of Monmouth by way of his best-selling book *The History of the Kings of Britain*, written in 1135. He later wrote *The Life of Merlin*, which dealt with Merlin and his retreat into the Caledonian forest where he lived in isolation, but for the company of animals. Geoffrey of Monmouth drew upon the poems attributed to the historic Welsh bard Myrddin as well as local traditions surrounding the figure, and he then changed the name to Merlin. Like Taliesin (see the Hierophant card), Myrddin was a sixth-century Welsh bard who migrated to the north of what is now England. Most of the poems attributed to him are contained in the collection known as The Black Book of Carmarthen and, while considered too late to be the authentic writings of Myrddin, they could have derived from earlier original works of the poet. The prophecies of Myrddin which make up a part of these writings are, however, deemed to be additions made by later scribes and not the words of the prophet, as the text reflects the political scene of the twelfth century onward.

Merlin appears in *The History of the Kings of Britain* as the boy who has to prove himself at a young age. The reckless King Vortigern had taken refuge in Wales from the invading Saxons, whom he had, by way of his policy, enabled to gain a foothold in Britain. He planned to build a fortress at Dinas Emrys, but each morning would wake to find the work of the previous day in ruins. Vortigern's druids told him the building needed a sacrifice and the blood of a fatherless boy to be sprinkled over the foundations for the structure to stand. Merlin was rumoured to be the son of the devil and thus was brought before the king as a fatherless child. But the gifted, farseeing boy challenged the druid's theory, explaining that if they were to dig down into the ground below the site they would find two dragons who fought each night and thus were the cause of the destruction. A crew began to dig and found the dragons as described—one red and the other white—which, the boy went on to explain, represented the Britons and Saxons respectively, and their forthcoming battles.

The character and fate of Myrddin contrasts that of the magician of Arthurian romance who retains an air of pagan woodland, yet still enjoys a comfortable existence at court as the protector and adviser of Arthur and his Round Table. Being that the Merlin of Arthur's court is well known, we shall take the opportunity here to visit the men who are thought to have been the inspiration behind the magician. The character of Myrddin, who is Geoffrey's source and rooted in history, lived a solitary life (but for his pet pig and wolf) in the Caledonian forest. He suffered a madness and took to muttering prophecies after his traumatic experience on the battlefield of Arderydd, which left deep psychic wounds. Geoffrey's Merlin likewise takes flight to the wild after a dreadful battle in the north in which three of his companions are killed. He finds safety and calm in the forest, where he likes to hide in the cover of an apple tree, believing he is a hunted man. In time he is found beside a spring and subdued with music and taken back to the court where there was interest in his prophecies. But society and its crowds cause him to panic, madness reclaims him, and he returns to his wood-wild state. Merlin stays in his beloved forest but for one public appearance, that being the wedding of his ex-wife, where he arrives riding a stag, with a herd of deer as a wedding gift. The groom laughs at the sight, and on impulse Merlin kills him with a pair of antlers. He is then captured and put on display, where his prophetic utterances prove true. After his release he returns to the forest, which begins to heal him. His prophecies echo creation myths and his personal experience by their cycle of destructive horrors, then profound calm, then renewal. He asks his sister to build a forest dwelling designed for scientific and prophetic observation of the stars that will also provide shelter from the winter. Taliesin visits him for long, esoteric conversations, and a new spring is found from which Merlin drinks, bathes, and is healed of distress. Society wishes his return but he refuses, choosing to live out his life in his forest sanctuary in pursuit of wisdom with Taliesin, Ganieda (a friend of his sister), and a second unfortunate wild man, whom Merlin leads to the spring and restoration.

There are two further figures whose stories are thought to mingle with and mirror that of Myrddin.

The first is named Lailoken, who is found in the wood naked and hairy by St. Kentigern, patron saint of Glasgow. He fought in a terrible battle on the same field as Arderydd and there saw the sky open up and riders form in the clouds to threaten and accuse him of being responsible for the carnage, after which the spirits drove him from the field into the cover of the forest, where he lived wild with the animals. It was his habit to sit upon a rock and deliver his prophecies so as to interrupt the services of St. Kentigern. He foretold his own death at the hands of shepherds, which is an important passage in the manuscript, for it also identifies him with Merlin: "Merlin is said to have met a triple death" (Tolstoy, *Quest for Merlin*)—that is, by stone, stake, and water.

Lastly, there is the sad Irish tale known as "the Frenzy of Suibhne," where King Suibhne is seized by battle panic and flies (literally) into the safety of the neighbouring treetops, and then lives out his life roaming lonely landscapes, living on wild cresses and water, until his death by the spear of a jealous husband whose wife had kindly been leaving milk for the lost soul. Suibhne also had his skirmishes with the church, namely St. Ronan, who some said brought the madness on by a curse. In vying for public favour, the churchmen began to claim the same mantic gifts and affinity with the wild as the pagan wood-wild men—a sign of the begrudging respect and competitive air between the seer and the saint.

UPRIGHT

Silence. Retreat. Withdrawing from the outside world. Protection and concealment. Calm soul-searching. Seeking wisdom and understanding of the larger patterns in life. Guidance or advice from an elder. Pilgrimage. Searching, wandering. A philosopher. Psychic abilities enhanced by peace and freedom of thought. Foresight. Prudence. Knowledge. A study and respect of nature and the limits it places upon us, such as the effects of seasons, time, etc. Reflection. Giving thought to one's self or condition. Leaving the material riches in search of the spiritual. Celibacy. Healing. Resolving serious problems. Recuperating. Valuing time alone. Taking time to lick one's wounds. Peace. The solitary nature of the Hermit card can be a positive or negative condition in one's life—on the positive side, solitary time can bring peace and clarity, a balancing, a sense of well-being, or transformation. On the other hand, it can be negative in isolating a person, creating misanthropy, and bringing on fear, fatigue, and depression and distancing one from real aspirations, dreams, opportunities, and good company. Check surrounding cards for an indication as to positive or negative influence.

REVERSED

Suffering. Exile. Persecution complex. Being held back by limited philosophies. Being stubborn and narrow. Misanthropy. Dismissing outside help or advice. Dangerous disregard for one's self and others. Fragile health. Loneliness. Starving for care and kindness. Depression brought on by isolation.

10: Wheel of Fortune

DESCRIPTION

The traditional tarot imagery has a woman dressed in fine robes entertaining herself with the spin of a wheel. Sometimes she wears a blindfold, other times she is led by her moods. Figures of animals or men ride the wheel (in this case, both), symbolizing the cyclical states of man: "I will reign, I reign, I have reigned, I am without."

Arianrhod

Arianrhod was daughter of Don and sister to Gwydion the magician. Her tale and character in the Mabinogion are a puzzling mix of base mortal behaviour and echoes of divine powers, which have to be understood as a consequence of Arianrhod having once been a goddess in the distant past, whose story has become diluted and confused over time. The Welsh Triads name her as one of the most beautiful women in Britain, and she is considered by some a goddess of dawn and/or stellar goddess. The constellation Corona Borealis is known to the Welsh as Caer Arianrhod and is, in turn, associated with the wheel of fate. The Caer ("castle") of Arianrhod is the name also given to a large reef rock formation which can be seen at very low tide off the coast near Llandwrog. The name Arianrhod means "silver wheel" or "queen of the wheel," which—together with her role of placing destinies upon Llew (albeit in this case cruel bindings)—led me to choose her to illustrate the Wheel of Fortune card. However, her role, as with much of the mythology, is open to speculation. With origins long lost we are left with fascinating and shadowy figures of whom we can see glimpses of their former glory, and yet they defy strict classification.

The fourth branch of the *Mabinogion* tells of how the great magician Math contended with a special requirement to life: except in time of war, he would have to sit with his feet resting in the lap of a virgin or he would cease to exist. (Also see the Magician card.) Arianrhod had been recommended by her brother Gwydion for the position of foot-holder. When Math asked if she was a maid, she replied she was. He then bent his wand and asked her to step over it as a test. Arianrhod slipped over the wand and there appeared, to great surprise, a fine, fair-haired boy. At the cry of the babe, Arianrhod made for the door in shame, and a second child was left in her wake, which Gwydion snatched up and hid in a chest. Math named the first boy Dylan Eil Ton ("son of the wave"), who took to the sea like a fish at his baptism and disappeared beneath the water. Gwydion quietly took the second son to a woman who could nurse the babe. He grew at twice the rate of a normal child and when he was four, Gwydion took him to meet his mother. Arianrhod was furious, accusing her brother of trying to disgrace her with the existence of the child. She asked the boy's name and, when told he had not been given one, she announced, "I lay a destiny upon him that he shall never have a name unless he receives one from me." Gwydion was disgusted, calling her a wicked woman, adding that her only affliction was that she was no longer called a damsel.

The next day Gwydion turned sedges and seaweed into a boat, then conjured some beautiful leather, disguised himself and the boy as shoemakers, and visited the port of Caer Arianrhod. In time, Arianrhod boarded the boat to have her foot measured. While in her view the boy took aim and hit a bird with a stone, to which she remarked on his skill. Gwydion had triumphed, for she unwittingly called the boy Llew Llaw Gyffes, "bright one of the skillful hand." Arianrhod's resolve only grew—"I will lay a destiny upon this boy that he shall never have arms and armour until invested by me." Gwydion vowed to overcome her malice.

Years passed. Llew became a fine figure of a young man, and he and Gwydion returned to Caer Arianrhod disguised as young bards. They were well received, feasted, and entertained in return. In the half light of dawn, Gwydion called his magic and raised a phantom navy and fighting force to lay siege to the castle. In a state of alarm, Arianrhod armed the two bards in defense of her castle. Once Llew stood in full battledress, Gwydion relaxed and called off the siege, explaining to Arianrhod that the tumult was only to surmount her prophecy and obtain arms for the boy. With fate twice cheated, Arianrhod laid a third and last destiny upon her son: that he would never have a wife of the race that now inhabits the earth, whereupon Gwydion unleashed his tongue, calling for none to support a woman of such malice. As the two left Arianrhod for the last time, Gwydion vowed Llew would have a wife despite her fateful bindings (see the Sun card).

UPRIGHT

Surprise. Change of fortune. Unexpected turn of events. Good luck. Progression. Windfall. Measurable time or natural cycle. Upturn of the wheel. Improvement. After struggles, obstacles give way and plans engage. Breakthrough and movement. Blind fortune. Chance. Moods of fate. Surmounting difficulties. Relief from another's oppression. The Wheel of Fortune can herald random change neither sought nor deserved, reminding us that fate sometimes rewards the unworthy while denying those deserving of luck. The card also carries a warning to the vain and fame seekers, in that what went up must come down, and at times depicts the figure atop the wheel with the ears of an ass. The wheel can represent a natural shift of circumstance or phase in life, such as the change from adolescent to adult, adult to middle age, etc.

REVERSED

Instability. Temporary fortune. Displacement and roaming. Hounding, demanding people or circumstances. Shifting fortunes make it difficult to set a course. Sheer bad luck born of simple chance.

11: Justice

DESCRIPTION

The traditional tarot imagery depicts a capable, poised woman holding scales to weigh and measure in one hand and a sword to implement or protect justice in the other. She wears rich robes and is sometimes partly armoured. Unlike the modern image of civil justice who wears a blindfold, the woman of the tarot card represents divine justice and therefore has full sight.

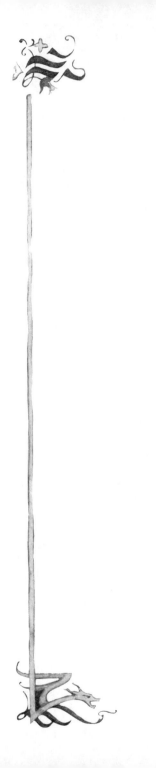

Lady of the Fountain

The preservation of justice was often touted as the first responsibility of a king. To rule well, one was required to be patient, of independent mind, protective of rights, charitable, and yet have the strength to uphold the law without mercy. Rather than a line of direct decent, the system of early Celtic kingship was dependent on merit and elective, with a suitable candidate being drawn from within the royal clan. The flexibility and strength of the system can be appreciated in that it allowed a poor prospect to be avoided, or a king challenged. Delving below Shakespeare's play Macbeth and into history, the actions taken by the northern Scottish king can be seen as acceptable within the Celtic system, even expected, as a native hero would be encouraged to champion the land and rid her of an unfit king. In brief, Mac Beth was a serious contender for the Scottish crown in both character and birth, since he carried the blood of two royal dynasties. However, Duncan came to the throne and proved a dismal king, particularly in the arena of war and defense. Mac Beth challenged the High King in battle whilst he traveled through Mac Beth's northern territory. Duncan later died of his wounds, leaving Mac Beth to lead Scotland into a long and prosperous reign.

There was the strong belief that the king and the land were bound in a sacred marriage, and that the country would prosper as a reflection of her "husband" so long as he was fit to rule in mind and body. If the hero-king were less than desirable, particularly physically afflicted, then it was believed the land would consequently suffer and become a wasteland, overrun by war and pestilence. The rightful king of

the land may prove himself by achieving a quest or perform-
ing an extraordinary feat, such as Arthur pulling the sword
from the stone, which was seen to be a supernatural sign of the
land having made her choice. The mythologies of Celtic countries often
personify the land into a woman and dramatize her search for a just and
capable king. The concept of the country personified carries through to the
modern day with the image of Britannia, who appears on British cur-
rency as a woman seated, helmed, with shield and trident. Sovereignty is
the title given to such a conceptual woman, and her image can differ
greatly, depending on the country's condition, mood, and season—she
may be a young, fertile maid of spring or a wizened crone of winter and
neglect. In mythology, she likes to haunt otherworldly intersections such
as fountains and mounds. She usually appears in her repulsive guise,
which she finds conducive to drawing out the truth from the would-be
champion, whose heart, wit, and physical prowess she has come to judge.

In the romances of the Mabinogion, Owaine, son of Urien, is
seen as a favourite of King Arthur's and having ties to the
Otherworld, as symbolized by the army of three hundred ravens
who are his companions and his reputation of never losing a battle. While at Arthur's court, he heard a tale told by the knight
Kynon of a mysterious, dangerous adventure to be had in finding a wild herdsman, an otherworldly tree and fountain, and
challenging its guardian Black Knight in combat. Kay unfairly
made sport of Owaine's interest in the tale, quipping that
Owaine's deeds did not match his tongue. With no word of his
plan, young Owaine left the court at dawn in search of the
fabled fountain. He crossed mountains and deserts to arrive at
the castle he had heard described as held by a man dressed in
yellow. He was well received, and though the yellow
man seemed concerned for Owaine's welfare, he

told him how to proceed, and the next morning Owaine set out in search of the Black Man of the glade. (See also the Horned One card.) Owaine found the formidable character seated upon a mound, surrounded by wild animals whom he guarded and controlled. As Kynon had described, he was an awesome sight, being a titanic black giant (assuming black from not having bathed), having only one leg and one eye, and being attended by herds of animals that orbited him like stars. He carried a club, and while he enjoyed being rough and uncivil to the questing heroes, he did advise Owaine on how to find the miraculous tree and its fountain. The tree was larger than Owaine could have imagined. Beneath its great boughs he found the fountain, a marble slab, and a silver bowl affixed by a silver chain. As the Black Man had instructed, Owaine filled the bowl with water and spilled it over the marble. A peal of thunder tore open the sky and a shower of rain and hail poured down so violent as to tear the flesh and cause Owaine to fear for his life. The skies then cleared to reveal a beaten landscape and the tree stripped of all its leaves. A flock of birds then came to roost in the bare branches and sang a song, sweet and exotic, unlike any Owaine had ever heard. The music had a power that set a mood of bliss upon him, only to be broken by the commotion raised by the charge of the Black Knight who burst upon the valley. The knight, horse, and lance were clothed in a rich black velvet that billowed and snapped at the high speed. Owaine prepared himself and the two collided with great force, breaking both their lances. Swords were drawn and as the battle wore on, the Black Knight suffered a serious head wound and, clinging to life, turned his horse for home. Owaine followed to see him enter a splendid castle, and raced to make the gate, but horrifically the portcullis came down upon Owaine's horse just behind the saddle, killing his horse, shaving his spurs, and leaving him trapped by the inner gate. A woman watched him a while, weighing him and finally deeming him worthy of rescue. Luned was her name, and in her outspoken manner she told him that all women ought to succour him and that she believed him faithful in the service of women, a sincere friend, and a devoted lover. She then gave him a ring with the power to make him invisible and stole the prisoner to her chambers. From her window, Owaine caught his first sight of the countess amidst the funeral procession of her husband the Black Knight, who had succumbed to the wound Owaine had inflicted. Grief had changed her golden beauty to a disheveled fright as she compulsively tore at her skin and bloodstained dress. Yet, despite worst appearance, Owaine's heart became inflamed with love for the Lady of the Fountain. Luned told him of her regal qualities and set about to woo her mistress on Owaine's behalf—for the good of the country and fountain, which needed a worthy guardian. However, it was no easy task to fool the countess. She held Owaine steadfast in her gaze, searched his eyes, and knew him to be the man who had chased the soul from the body of her lord. Again, Luned stepped forward and made her case to the countess. With steely cool reason, she argued that if Owaine was the challenger who had overthrown the

Black Knight, then so much the better, for the deed proved him the champion and best fit to defend the fountain and her realm. With no remedy for the past, the Lady of the Fountain took council with her subjects and weighed her options, deciding in favour of Owaine, who became her husband, defended the fountain, and earned his fame and the love of the realm. Three years passed before he was reunited with Arthur, and his story resumed with adventure, consequential neglect of his beloved lady, and then heroics to restore confidence and win her back.

UPRIGHT

Deliberating. Search for truth and justice. Weighing an issue or situation. Striving for balance and equilibrium. Remaining impartial or centered, and so capable of fair judgment. Insight. Honesty and honour. Discriminating logic. The value of order. The triumph of reason. Appropriate response. Karma. Law of cause and effect. Negotiating. Equal partnerships. Legal affairs. Favourable judgment in legal matters. Self-government. Having the inner strength and confidence not to be swayed by the opinions of others. Internal balance achieved by being temporarily unattached to an outcome. Having the patience to allow Justice time to determine Her course. Having the courage, strength, and conviction to uphold and implement justice. Taking the right action, even if unpopular or costly. The card can relate to civil justice or the concept of divine justice.

REVERSED

Injustice. Dishonesty. False charge or witness. Poor judgment. Prejudice. Denying the truth and real motivations. Cowardice. Forsaking justice. Abuse. Corruption. Obstruction of justice. Entanglement of legalities. Perversion of justice. Giving into popular opinion and forsaking truth. Past sins come home to roost.

12: The Hanged Man

DESCRIPTION

The traditional tarot imagery depicts a man hanging by one foot, or by the neck, with his hands bound. Often there are two pillars and a crossbeam, giving an impression of a doorway into another realm or of being once removed, marginalized. While the man is uncomfortable in his restriction, he does not wear an expression of pain; rather, he has a look of calm resignation, sometimes even amusement.

Enchantment
of Dyfed

The land of Dyfed was known to be susceptible to the influence of
the Otherworld, having shifting or overlapping boundaries between the
two realms. In the first branch of the Mabinogion, Pwyll, ruler of Dyfed,
unwittingly crosses the boundary (see the Death card) and befriends
Arawn, King of Annwn, and marries the otherworldy Rhiannon. In the
third branch, the unseen powers reach into this realm and envelop the
land of Dyfed . . .

One night an inexplicable peal of thunder traveled the
breadth of the land, followed by a dense, immobilizing
mist and silence. Dyfed was under a powerful enchantment
suspending the lives of all the inhabitants but four—Pryderi,
lord of Dyfed; his wife, Kicva; his mother, Rhiannon; and her
second husband, Manawydan. When the fog lifted, Dyfed
rested in an eerie silence, devoid of all people and their livestock, leaving only the wildlife to roam the land. Years passed
and the small family adjusted to their situation by hunting
and living off the land (also see the Chariot card). One day
Manawydan and Pryderi were hunting when a brilliant
white boar overtook them and led the hounds to a

grand, mysterious castle where none had stood before. Manawydan could feel the tightening grip of the unseen and cautioned Pryderi not to enter in pursuit of the boar. But Pryderi would not listen and went in after the hounds. Once inside, he found an ornate fountain and above it a beautiful golden bowl hanging by four blue chains that rose into the air with no end. Pryderi reached for the bowl and at once his hands stuck to the sides. A cold wave traveled up his arms and his limbs weighed like lead; he found himself paralyzed. Manawydan knew he would be no match for the power that gripped Dyfed and held his friend, and so waited outside until nightfall, then returned home. On learning of the mysterious events, Rhiannon was determined to find her son and against her husband's advice she entered the castle and met the same fate as Pryderi in reaching for the cauldron. A triumphant peal of thunder ripped through the sky and with it the castle and prisoners vanished. For seven years mother and son remained suspended between worlds, immobilized in their frozen state, unable to even mutter a word.

Manawydan and Kicva lived on alone, not knowing whether they would see their partners again. In thinking of their survival, Manawydan tried an experiment in cultivating the land and sowing wheat in three fields. He tended with care and the venture was a great success. The eyes of the unseen were also attracted to swaying seas of wheat and thus could not help but reap mischief. Manawydan prepared his first field for harvest, but the next day arrived to find not one stalk of wheat standing—all having been gnawed half mast and ears ravished. The following day he met the same sight in his second field. The third night he hid within the verge to witness a legion of mice descend upon the crop. There were so many mice in the raiding party that all at once each and every stalk bowed with the weight of a mouse. Manawydan rushed upon the field, finding them as difficult to catch as gnats. But he did manage to grab one of the culprits, whom he placed in his glove and cinched the opening with a string. On returning home, he hung the glove on a peg by the fire and Kicva inquired after what was inside. He replied, "A thief, and tomorrow I will hang the mouse for its crime." Kicva objected to his plan, as it was unseemly for a man of his dignity to be seen hanging rodents. But Manawydan was adamant; the mouse had robbed him and would swing at the end of the rope. On the following day he set about building the tiny gallows when a priest approached (to Manawydan's satisfaction, as he was the first person to be seen in Dyfed in years). The priest asked what he was doing and he replied that he was hanging a creature that had robbed him. The priest went on to try to buy the life of the mouse, but Manawydan refused the offer. The priest left and in his place arrived a bishop just as the noose was drawn up around her neck. Manawydan was unflinching and eventually the bishop asked him to name his price— which was the return of Pryderi and Rhiannon and the spell to be lifted from Dyfed, with the promise of no more retaliation and an explanation as to the events. We then learn the identity of the bishop, who is in fact a magician

of considerable power who was a friend to Gwawl, the suitor of Rhiannon, whom Pwyll (Pryderi's father) had cruelly beaten in a game called "Badger in the Bag." The charm upon the land and family had been revenge for Gwawl's past suffering. And as for the identity of the precious mouse—she was in fact the wife of the magician, who together with her ladies in waiting had asked to join the raid in the shape of a mouse. But being pregnant, she hadn't the nimble movement needed to escape Manawydan's reach.

UPRIGHT

Restraint. Suspension. Stalemate. Atonement. Not being able to make one's influence felt. Being held at a disadvantage. The dull pain born of constraint. Being caught in a web. A freeze on life. Detachment and isolation. Impotence and chastisement. Can mean a punishment, as in the law of retaliation applying to the traitor. Such suspensions can follow betraying one's self in doing or allowing something in one's life that was known to be wrong. Feeling marginalized, which can be a form of protection. Redemption. The silence of constraint brings deeper self-knowledge and sharpens the intuitive senses—as a blind man "sees." Tapping a deep root. Uncommon knowledge. A life pared down to the basics. A time of gestation in a borderland state between chapters in life. Self-sacrifice in pursuit of knowledge or a cause. Energy drain. Delays and suspension of plans. A wise temporary surrender. Endurance. Insight. Being still in order to learn the secret to freeing one's self.

REVERSED

Futile attempts to revive something past. Thwarted efforts. Illusion. Blind shoots that do not flower. Not knowing when it is wise to surrender. Unrealistic expectations. Disappointment and delusion. Ego. Martyr of an unworthy cause. Missing the point of a lesson.

13: Death

DESCRIPTION

The traditional tarot imagery of the Death card varies from a skeleton mowing communities, as in the manner of the plague, to a mounted figure with a scythe cutting down individual representatives of the differing social classes, symbolizing death as the great leveller of society. Other decks are of a quiet tone, depicting Death as a calm skeleton hunter, sometimes bandaged and equipped with bow and arrow.

Arawn

The first branch of the Mabinogion begins with the tale of Pwyll, lord of Dyfed, and his meeting with Arawn, lord of Annwn, and his spectral hounds. Annwn means "otherworld" or "underworld," but is not to be confused with the concept of hell; rather, it is a plane more evolved than ours where ancestors reside. Arawn's rival in Annwn is a king named Hafgan, meaning "summer white," leaving some to speculate that the two kings personify the seasons and so regularly battle to reign over the land. South Wales has another ruler of the Underworld in Gwyn ap Nudd, who leads the spectral Wild Hunt through the sky, collecting souls of the dead. Each year on the first of May, Gwyn ap Nudd battles his rival, Gwythyr ap Greidawl, for the maiden Creiddylad. She spends half the year with one, then the other, and is thought to represent the land in the grip of the seasons in their cycle of death and rebirth.

Pwyll was hunting in the area of Glyn Cuch when he lost his companions after following the hounds into the woods. As he gave chase there came the baying of hounds, but unlike his own, from the opposite direction. The woods then opened into a glade where Pwyll saw the unworldly hounds bring down a stag. Their coats shone an illuminous white and their ears glistened red. Pwyll drove off the hounds and set his own upon the stag, at which time a horseman on a fine dapple-grey mount entered the glade. He was a most dignified figure, dressed in shades of grey, with a fine hunting horn around his neck. He rebuked Pwyll for having denied his hounds their prize in favour of his own and warned that if he chose to take revenge it would bring more dishonour than the value of a hundred stags. Pwyll conceded and asked if there were a way he could make amends and win his friendship. The horseman introduced himself as Arawn, a king of Annwn, and explained that he had a rival king in Annwn named Hafgan, who was ever provoking him into war. Arawn asked if Pwyll would exchange places with him for one year, taking each other's semblance and ruling in each other's stead. At the end of the year it was customary for Arawn and Hafgan to meet in single combat at the ford of a river to decide the lordship of Annwn. And so Pwyll, if he agreed to the switch, would be fighting Hafgan on behalf of Arawn, disguised as Arawn, with no one to know his true identity. The king further warned Pwyll to make his first blow count and not to take a second, for as Arawn had learned in the past, with one blow Hafgan would die, but two blows and he would miraculously resurrect to return fit the next day to fight anew. Pwyll agreed to the adventure and the two set out for each other's realms, agreeing to meet again in the glade in a year and a day.

Pwyll marveled at the beauty of Annwn, the castle, and its queen. As a mark of respect for Arawn, Pwyll resisted her for the year that he shared her bed, and his was time passed in comfort.

The battle with Hafgan unfolded as Arawn foretold and though Pwyll's first blow was effective it did not kill

Hafgan outright. He pleaded for a second blow and release, but Pwyll (as Death) would not oblige, remembering death was the key to his rejuvenation. Hafgan was taken away by his men and the triumphant Pwyll set about uniting Annwn under the reign of Arawn. By the following day all was set, and he met once again with Arawn, who was most relieved to hear of Pwyll's success. As a measure of his gratitude, he bestowed the title of "Head of Annwn" upon Pwyll. The respect deepened when Arawn learned from his perplexed wife that she had not known his love in the preceding year. Likewise, on Pwyll's return to Dyfed, he was told that never had his rule been so wise as the previous year. Arawn sent him the coveted gift of otherworldly swine and the two kings remained fast friends, generous and loyal in each other's aid.

UPRIGHT

Evolution. Change, death, and transformation. A natural end to a situation, whether it be positive or negative; for example, the card may refer to the end of a relationship, illusion, financial source, or the completion of a project. Closure. Releasing of the past. The end of an era. Necessary change. Freedom that allows for renewal. Sudden change brings fears of the unknown, but ultimately alters life in such a way as to initiate new growth. May mean death, a fear of death, or a brush with death. Natural course and progression of life. Lastly, Death is sometimes portrayed as a beautiful and dignified figure since dying can be seen as a blessing in release from suffering.

REVERSED

Stagnation. Avoiding the risk of change brings depression and decay. Unhealthy delay. Serious illness. Immobility. Extended suffering. Illusion. Being held back by the dead atmosphere of a place or attitude of its people. Extended grieving or denial of loss.

14: Temperance

DESCRIPTION

The traditional tarot imagery is that of a supernatural woman or angel who stands with one foot in water and the other on land, to symbolize being of or bridging two worlds. She pours water from one vessel into another, as in the (tempering) custom of mixing water and wine.

Keeper
of the Well

Legend says that beneath the waters of Cardigan Bay lies the submerged kingdom of the Cantre'r Gwaelod, or "bottom hundred." Fishermen claim that on bright days one can still see its ghostly ruins casting shadows on the ocean floor. (There are unusual features to the seabed in this area which have likely given rise to the legend; modern investigators, however, believe them to be natural formations.) Cantre'r Gwaelod was once a fertile plain supporting sixteen towns before the waters rose in the sixth century to swallow a span of land measuring forty miles long and twenty wide. The more recent, popular accounts of the story are but a pale shade when compared with the dramatic, foreboding atmosphere of the early legend. The simplified (and sanitized) latter versions tell of how the land was protected from the sea by an embankment of stone and sluices. Gwyddno Garanhirs, lord of the realm, entrusted the care of the embankment to a man named Seithennin, who was a notorious drunk among an already indulgent population. Seithennin left his duties to his assistants, who left them to theirs, who left the wall to itself and thus to decay. One night a banquet was held, and Seithennin being "in his cups" left the sluices open, and the sea raged in to conquer the land and its people in one dreadful night.

The darker depth and substance of the earlier legend can be felt through the vague but powerful ninth-century poem contained in The Black Book of Carmarthen. It is a short poem, classed as a speech-poem, that would have provided only a part of the legend *when recited by a bard in performance. As such, the poem leaves many unanswered questions as to the identity of the narrator, characters, and what crimes brought on the waters. The drive of the story and some of its lost details can be recovered from the sister or parallel tales found in Ireland and Brittany. In following the example of the sister tales and piecing together fragments of Welsh tradition with the poem, we can gain a reconstructed view as to the likely course of the lost tale…*

Seithennin was known to be a man of intemperance, presumption, and indolence, who had earned a reputation as being one of the three drunkards of the Isle of the Mighty (Britain). One night after a feast he left the hall and either sought out or stumbled upon the young girl who was guardian or keeper of the well. (The well is sometimes termed a "faery well," and so the girl was likely the priestess of a sacred well.) Not knowing any limits to his behaviour, Seithennin then violated the girl, whose cries rose to pierce the night air. The waters of the well then rose to rage and drown the land and its people. All perished but the keeper of the fountain, who continued to live on in the quiet and safety of the depths of the sea.

The surviving source poem contained in The Black Book of Carmarthen has subtle shifts in translation. It has also been interpreted differently; for example, blaming the girl's curiosity or unidentified and unwarranted anger for the inundation. While such theories may be correct, neither explains the cries and complaint of the girl, why her voice haunts the narrator, or the refrain of guilt driving the poem. In keeping with the dramatic heights of the tale, I would even venture to suggest the well rose of its own accord to avenge the rape of its priestess after her imploring to God, and not as is the usual view that it overflowed in her neglect while she fought off her attacker. The opening verse calls Seithennin forth to look upon the destructive waters. It then continues on to accuse the girl, as cup bearer of the fountain, of unleashing the raging waters after her complaint. The poem effectively contrasts the wild cries of the girl, which return on the wind and keep the narrator from sleep, with a moral refrain that surges in a steady, wavelike rhythm to caution what fate will follow presumption and excess. The poem is laden with the air of guilt and repentance. The Black Book of Carmarthen is also quoted in translation as stating "Seithennin had violated a young girl who tended a magic well, which then overflowed and flooded the lands of Gwyddneu" (Markale, *Women of the Celts*). Similar crimes were also committed by a king named Amangons, who with his companions raped the young guardians of wells and stole their golden cups.

Irish tradition preserves a close parallel tale in the creation of Lough Ree and Lough Neagh, which are said to cover the lands of King Ecca. The area had a magic well within a small garden surrounded by a thick wall. After prophecies of flooding, the king set a girl to guard the well, who is assumed to have been his daughter Libane. One night she neglected to cover the well, which overflowed to drown the entire kingdom and all inhabitants except Libane and her beloved dog, who continued to live on in the depths of the lake. A later tradition says a hundred years passed and Libane made a wish; thereafter she turned into a

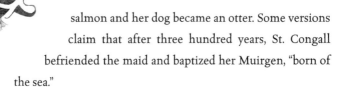

salmon and her dog became an otter. Some versions claim that after three hundred years, St. Congall befriended the maid and baptized her Muirgen, "born of the sea."

Lastly, Breton tradition preserves another branch of the tale in what looks to be the remnants of a powerful and popular pagan priestess who becomes the scapegoat of her Christianized father, in the legend of Kers-Ys, "city of depths." During the fifth century a king named Gradlon gave the city to his daughter Dahud, whose old pagan ways and wild lifestyle provoked condemnation and hostilities from the new Christian religion. Along with the fellow citizens of the Kers-Ys, Dahud was reputed to have loose morals and an insatiable sexual appetite. The town was protected from the sea by a dyke and locked gates, the keys to which were worn around Dahud's neck. Other versions state they were jealously guarded by Gradlon, leaving Dahud to steal the keys at the urging of her lover. Sin was said to cause the surrounding sea to rise up and inundate the town. St. Gwenole warned Gradlon of the oncoming catastrophe, and he made his escape on horseback. Dahud tried to save herself by climbing up behind her father, but at the command of a voice telling him to cast off the devil, he chose to forsake his daughter and left her to drown. Another version says St. Gwenole held a cross to Dahud's forehead until her strength waned, leaving the waves and undertow to claim her. Gradlon survived; so too did Dahud—according to the fishermen who claim to have seen her swimming as a mermaid with great schools of fish amidst the drowned cityscape of Kers-Ys.

UPRIGHT

Tempering. Moderation. Adaptation. Managing a volatile situation in a calm, thoughtful way. Grace under pressure. Healing. Balance, reflection, and patience. Having clear boundaries. A confident and outspoken survivor. Bridging two very different worlds. The successful mixing of two opposites. Combining materials. This tarot card is sometimes called the Art card and speaks of visionary art that brings ideas from one world to the next. Being of two worlds. Ability to adapt. Beneficial transformation. Successful combination of ideas, lifestyles, or people. Creating a nurturing, appropriate environment. Caring for one's health. Repose. Feeling protected and removed. Guardian angel. Self-control. Compatibility. Blending and harmony. Finding inner peace. A period of waiting and constructive use of time.

REVERSED

Excess, pride, impatience. Rash behaviour. Indulgence. Unworkable unions. Uncondusive environment. A fish out of water. Incompatibility. Irreconcilable differences. Inability to adapt. Impulsive behaviour. Exacerbating a difficult situation. Regret.

15: The Horned One

DESCRIPTION

The imagery of the traditional Devil card depicts a large goatlike figure, part man, part beast, with hairy pelt and cloven hooves, which, as explained in the following section, is a description of the spirit of the wild or god of the hunt, whose image became a convenient scapegoat assigned to represent the devil of the incoming Christian religion. As the Devil, the card usually depicts two enslaved figures at the foot of the card, bound and hopeless, with the devil raising one

hand in a mock blessing. The decks that feature the Horned One instead of the devil depict a pastoral god with horns, sometimes attended by animals, other times by a lusty couple; the difference being that there are no chains or pain in the scene, only life in its natural state.

The Wild Herdsman

Before Christianity triumphed in Britain, the Horned God was an important figure as lord and protector of animals and god of the hunt. The delicate ecological balance between man and his environment was the charge of the Horned One, and since lives could depend on his favour, his worship was particularly difficult for Christianity to eradicate. It is not surprising, then, that the image of the nature-based Horned God conveniently became the image of the devil for the incoming Christian religion. Part man, part beast, hairy pelt, cloven hooves, dressed in animal skins and often horned and larger than life—these describe the personification of the spirit of the woods and wild, known under such names as the Horned One, Cernunnos, Wild Herdsman, Herne the Hunter, the Woodsward, Pan, Piper of the Dawn, etc. His appearance was meant to symbolize the integration of the animal cunning, strengths, and senses with the human consciousness and culture, resulting in a supernatural, supreme being of acute animal instinct and human intellect. Christianity never fully succeeded in rooting out the Horned One, who has been retained in tradition and folklore with varying degrees of human, animal, and godlike qualities. Though demoted from a god, he survives in legend and romance as an archetypal guardian and protector of animals, and in folklore as a personification of nature. He may also represent a temporary state of being, such as rebellion under pressure or returning to nature, as Merlin did in his flight to the wilderness where he spent years in a wood-wild state (also see the Hermit card). The Wild Herdsman may seem a common shepherd on first encounter, but the tales usually preserve remnants of his past glory and clues to his awesome powers. Such details include him preferring to sit cross-legged, in the traditional Horned God posture, upon a mound from where he can survey the surrounding forests or open land. He has animal attendants, with the stag, wolf, and boar being favourites, and herds of animals beyond, all of whom are under his control and protection. His appearance can range from representing the harsh season and unsympathetic side of nature in the form of the beastly, barbaric giant with wilting breath to the slender, vegetarian, human form donning antlers or branches and animal skins to represent the agility and grace also found in the wild.

In writing about the character of Merlin in the twelfth century, Geoffrey of Monmouth drew from history, tradition, poetry, and imagination, and has the prophet experience the subtle dance between genius and madness. For further discussion see the Hermit card, but in brief Merlin is overcome with a battle madness and flees the battlefield of Arderydd to live out his life in the isolation of the Caledonian forest. Given his mantic powers, it has been suggested that the character actually hears the call of the wild and takes cover in the woods, where the seeming simplicity of the wild can heal him as he distances himself from the trauma and cleans the psychic lesions left by battle. In gentle contemplation of nature and his place within it, Merlin is able to shed his persona and rise anew. On first entering the forest, Merlin is wood-wild, foraging for roots, grass, berries, etc. with a herd of animals. He has an affinity with the creatures, who willingly do his bidding. An old wolf and pig are his loyal companions, and he was known to ride a stag, wear antlers, and drive a herd of deer. A similar character named Suibhne Geilt of Irish tradition was known to ride in the antlers of a stag whilst it drew a plough. Also Irish, and wild, was Tuan Mac Cairill, who lived in a cave and suffered the cold in having only a thin covering of hair. He claimed that one evening when weak and injured, he felt a peculiar sensation come over him as antlers began to grow from his forehead. Soon after, his whole body began to shift into the shape of a young, healthy stag—a form that Tuan said brought him great joy. (A lively and in-depth study of such characters can be found in Nikolai Tolstoy's book *Quest for Merlin*.) It should be noted that while such figures suffered mental distress or illness, they are not to be confused with the more common, unfortunate wild men who lived largely outside society, having low intelligence and little language, and who were often frightened, aggressive, and overly sexual. The Wild Herdsman and Horned God derivatives, in contrast, were highly intelligent, cunning, sensitive, even artistic; they were also, appropriately, given their charge, vegetarian.

The Wild Herdsman appears in the *Mabinogion* in the tale of Kilhwch and Olwen. The band of heroes find him seated on a mound overlooking an otherworldly plain and tending a never-ending flock of sheep. He is a giant dressed in skins and accompanied by a dog the size of a horse. His name is Custennin and it is said that no animal had ever been lost to him, such was his care. But he cared less for the welfare of man and enjoyed taunting and challenging the questing knights: "Fools of men that they are!" (*Mabinogian*, tr. Guest).

The Lady of the Fountain, also contained within the collection of the *Mabinogion*, preserves another encounter with the formidable herdsman, where he is known as the Black Man— likely on account of the accumulation of dirt in living on the wild side rather than his actual skin colour. He is found seated upon a mound in a clearing of trees, and around him a great number of animals graze and doze. He is of immense size, has one eye, and holds a club. The knight Kynon greets him, but the herdsman cannot bring himself to be civil. Kynon asks after his power over the animals, and the man strikes his attending stag with the club, who then bellows, drawing all kinds of wildlife to the mound, so numerous as to be likened to the stars. The herdsman enjoys being disagreeable and rough with the knight, whom he calls "little man." Yet the hero has the courage to ask his intended question and the herdsman cooperates, advising the knight on how to find the otherworldly tree and what wondrous strange adventure he can expect to find there. (Also see the Justice card.)

UPRIGHT

Nature. The call of the wild. Animal impulse and instinct. Primal knowledge. Ancestral memory. Tension between order and chaos. Reconciling the cultured vs. natural state of being. Originality. Desire and fertility. Enchantment, fascination, and magnetism. Healthy competition. The integration of animal behaviour and needs with the civilized conscious. The rise of primal instincts such as nesting, nurturing, herding, and protecting. The attuning of animal qualities and senses, which can be of great value in agility, cunning, and the intuition of threats or unnatural conditions. The wisdom of the subconscious making its influence felt via one's appetites and aversions. Nature has a cycle and rhythm to regulate our behaviours, keeping balance and order. If oppression, starvation, or cruelty disrupt this order, then abhorrent, chaotic, self-destructive behaviour can ensue, leading to the traditional interpretation of the Devil card that appears in many decks as card number fifteen, indicating controlling relationships, enslaving obsession, violence, abuse, and addictions. However, unless a negative interpretation is suggested by surrounding cards, the Horned One of this deck is a symbol of a healthy, life-enhancing wild nature.

REVERSED

Imbalance. The destructive, upsetting force in the universe. Panic. Appetite with no conscience. Evil. Violence, perversion, and depravity. Oppression and weakness. The use of religion, virtue, and guilt as a weapon. Self-flagellation. Poor choices. Blind jealousy.

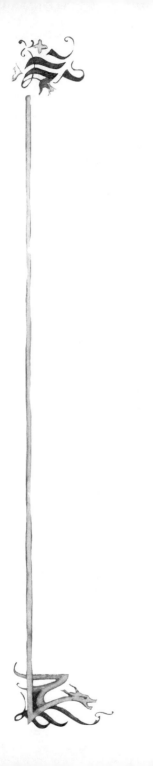

16: The Tower

DESCRIPTION

The traditional imagery of the tarot has the Tower as symbol of man's pride, arrogance, and ostentation. The tower cracks and collapses under the assault of lightning or fire above and waves of water below. Sometimes people are seen falling or leaping from the tower. The lightning represents divine punishment for greed, and the waves blast and level, symbolically cleansing the scene of corruption.

Bala Lake

One of the favourite themes in Welsh legend is that of the inundation tale in which towns and surrounding lands are drowned by the sea or a well which has been neglected or offended (see also the Temperance card). The tale of Llyn Tegid, or Bala Lake, is a fine example, having its roots in the old tradition of a well being the cause. It was said that the townspeople forgot to cover their well one night, which rose to swallow the site, leaving a lake three miles long and one wide. On calm, bright days, chimneys are said to be seen in the depths and bell chimes have been known to rise to the surface. The latter version of the tale belongs to the "water and warnings" branch of tradition, as it employs water as the instrument of destruction in punishment for greed, arrogance, pride, etc. Legend says that on still nights a voice skips over the surface of Bala Lake warning "vengeance will come" in an echo of the valley's traumatic past…

Long ago the valley was a lush, fertile land home to a cruel prince known for injustice and greed. He feared no man or god and was said to be so hated by the people of the surrounding parishes that his name stank in their nostrils. After the locals had muttered many prayers of deliverance, the winds of change began to shift and a voice warned the prince that "vengeance will come." But he scoffed and took no heed, seeing no reason to change his ways when

reprisal had not visited before. On the birth of his first son, the prince planned a celebration feast on an opulent, grand scale to impress the nobles of neighbouring lands. Many declined the invitation, yet others could not resist the spectacle and chance to serve their own interests at his table. A humble harper had been hired for the evening, and as he made his way down into the valley he thought he heard a voice on the evening breeze warning of vengeance to come. He cast his eyes about the landscape but could only see a little bird in amongst the hedgerow and so continued on his way. The feast was a splendid affair with all manner of meat and drink. The harper performed his duties and as the night wore on the crowd fell into a drunken free-for-all, forcing the humble harper to retreat to a quiet corner. As he sat alone watching the spectacle, a little bird entered the hall and hovered above the harp, whispering "Vengeance, vengeance." Repeatedly the bird warned until eventually the harper moved to follow its lead out of the hall. But the bird did not relax and harried him to quicken his pace, leading the bard deep into the night as a storm brewed, rumbled, and rallied in the distance. Once the bird had brought him to the height of a neighbouring hill, the storm bore down on the valley with all its might, forcing the harper to take shelter in a hedge. The rains cut and the wind tore up the turf, but when the deafening night had passed, the sun rose in a clear sky. The harper was in awe to see a large, serene lake now resting in the valley, leaving no trace of the court or its towers, only a harp rocking on the water's surface.

UPRIGHT

Destruction. Major change. Unheeded warnings. Greed, pride, arrogance. Revolution. Breakdown or breakthrough—the positive or negative implications of the card depend on the querent's position. If one has been living under oppression, dramatic and possible traumatic change will be freedom, but if one has been living the high life off the toil of others, expect reversal of fortune and loss. Irrepressible tantrum of change. Eruption. Triumph over enslaving, compulsive behaviours such as addiction or obsessive complexes. Collapse of the old system or lifestyle. Destruction of gains made by ill means. Clearing of the air. Cleansing destruction. Change of values.

REVERSED

Calamity. Disorganization. Danger, panic, crowding. Being trapped in an unhealthy lifestyle. Feeling of being entombed—alive but not participating in life. Lack of confidence and opportunity. An atmosphere of fear and restriction so strict as to be abusive.

17: The Star

DESCRIPTION

The traditional tarot imagery features a woman naked or dressed in blue, the colour of the exalted woman, i.e., Venus. She sits aside a pool of water that gives a reflective, meditative feel to the card and is suggestive of the treasures of the subconscious and life force. Two flasks appear, with one spilling water upon the ground, representing purpose and life force. She may have one foot in the water and one resting on land, as with the Temperance card. A calm, clear night sky crowns the scene and gives hope with the light of an eight-pointed star.

Branwen

Branwen was the daughter of Llyr and sister to the giant Bran the Blessed and Manawydan. Tradition names her as one of the three ancestresses or matriarchs of the Isle of the Mighty (Britain). Her dignified, resourceful character and tragic tale have given her a special place in the hearts of her countrymen. Branwen is ever the brave, considerate queen who suffers a dynastic marriage as a woman symbolic of her country. She makes much effort to guard the peace between two countries, but is thwarted by the hot tempers and posturing of the men that surround her. Branwen has two half brothers—Efnisien, meaning "not peaceful" or "strife," and Nisien, meaning "peaceful," who sadly plays a lesser role in her life, leaving her to die of a broken heart. Tradition places her grave on the banks of the river Alaw on the Isle of Anglesey, where a landmark burial mound may still be seen today. While Branwen's story ends tragically, it is her patience, enduring hope, and creative approach to surviving and ending her imprisonment that I wish to highlight in illustrating Star card qualities. Her "star," in this case a starling, was a source of comfort, hope, and help. In Celtic tradition birds are seen as otherworldly messengers, making the pair, in my view, a graceful example of the exalted air and higher mindset of the Star card.

Matholwch, king of Ireland, sailed to Harlech to ask Bran the Blessed, ruler of the Isle of the Mighty, for the hand of his sister Branwen in marriage. Bran took council and it was agreed that the marriage would benefit both countries. Branwen's half brother Efnisien, however, was not consulted, and after the wedding he cruelly mutilated the horses of the Irish king in spite. It was a terrible act, leaving Bran quick to compensate and repair relations. This was not an easy task, but the Irish were eventually appeased with the gift of a magic cauldron that had originally come from a lake in Ireland and had the power to restore life to a man, though he would not regain his speech. Matholwch and Branwen returned to Ireland and for one year all was well, with the queen enjoying friendship and honour and the birth of their son Gwern. But soon after, Matholwch's foster brothers began to brood over the insult of Efnisien and pressured the king to drive Branwen into the kitchen to serve the court as reprisal for the sins of her brother. There she cooked and toiled and was made to suffer a blow to the head each day at the hand of the butcher, on orders from above. Furthermore, no travel or trade was allowed between the Britons and Irish, lest word of the queen's abuse should reach her kinsman. Branwen bravely suffered her humiliation, keeping her heart warm by rearing a starling, which she kept hidden in a kneading trough. She taught the bird to speak and told it of her woes and the nature of her brother. Once the fair weather came and the starling was strong enough, Branwen tied a message of her plight to the root of its wing and asked it to find her brother. The brave little bird crossed the sea, finding Bran in Arvon, where it alighted on his shoulder and ruffled its feathers so the note would be seen. Bran was deeply distressed at the news and a host rallied about the giant, who led them onto Ireland and war. When the swineherds saw them approach the Irish coast, they reported to their lord that they saw a forest advance upon the sea and a mountain move alongside the wood. Branwen explained the riddle as the wood in reality being the yards and masts of ships, and the mountain her giant brother, whom no house could contain. The Irish retreated inland and offered to crown Branwen's son Gwern king of Ireland. But Bran refused to call off the advance. The Irish, thinking to honour him, built a house large enough to contain the giant. The gesture, together with Branwen's argument to spare both sides the devastation of war, caused Bran to relent. But alas, the house was a trap, hung with leather bags containing assassins. (Also see the Emperor card.) The plot was discovered by Efnisien, who in his typically savage way killed the would-be assassins and sat quietly to see the night unfold. All was congenial until Efnisien perceived a slight from the young Gwern, at which point he threw the boy headlong into the fire. It was a horrific scene as Branwen was restrained from the merciless flames and outrage erupted, with all sides falling into battle. The horror drew on as the Irish restored their dead in the very same cauldron Bran had given Matholwch. In view of the carnage, Efnisien repented and cast himself in the cauldron, which broke under his strain, as did his heart. The battle then turned in favour of the Britons, but when all was over only seven men survived to return home with Branwen. She is said to have stood upon Anglesey, looked in the direction of Ireland, then Wales, and, blaming herself for their destruction, died of sorrow, to be buried at the site in a four-sided grave now known as Branwen's Island.

UPRIGHT

Hope. Inspiration. Guiding star. Moment of grace and peace. Freedom. Early signs of life taking on a new pattern. Freedom after trials. Chance for escape. First sign of dawn. Release. Self-reliance. Clever, inspired ideas. Listening for direction. A quickening. Salvation. Empowerment. Destiny. A time of farseeing. Taking steps to save one's self—not giving into resignation. Enlightened idea. Planning. Thaw of the ice. Return of life force. Rejuvenation. Drawing strength from nature.

REVERSED

Resignation. Depression. No hope or energy. Allowing others to dictate one's life. Not listening to inner voice. Avoiding the quiet, dark time and so missing out on its wisdom. Consulting others when a creative solution lies deep inside one's own mind.

18: The Moon

DESCRIPTION

The traditional tarot imagery has the moon dominating the upper half of the card, with beams of light or dew descending to symbolize being under the influence of the moon. Two structures—towers or rock formations—flank the scene, giving the impression of a gateway or portal. Jackals or wolves usually represent the active nocturnal animal instincts, but here they are replaced with the owl of Blodeuwedd's legend. Fish replace the crayfish traditionally seen at the

foot of the card, representing the rising, primordial impulse of life. The water and its tides are symbolic of the subconscious and susceptible state of mind under the moon's influence.

Lake of Maidens

L lyn y Morynion, "Lake of Maidens," is a large lake that lies up high in the mountains of Ffestiniog. Two legends, if not more, have come to be associated with its dark waters, the first of which concerns the fate of Blodeuwedd, the wife of Llew Llaw Gyffes (also see the Sun card). The two great magicians Gwydion and Math had created Blodeuwedd from flowers to be the wife of Llew, whose mother had sworn he would never have a wife of the race that walked the earth. All had been well in the marriage until Blodeuwedd fell in love with Gronw Pebyr. Together they had plotted the murder of her husband, but their attempt only succeeded in severely wounding Llew. In the form of an eagle he went into hiding, to be found and rescued by Gwydion. Once healed, the two then returned to Ardudwy to avenge the crime and reclaim the land. At word of Gwydion's approach, Blodeuwedd and her maidens fled to the mountains. Distraught in their fear, they ran forever looking backward and, unaware of the dangers, fell into the lake. All but Blodeuwedd drowned in its depths. Gwyndion soon overtook her and, declaring he had a worse punishment for her crime, transformed her

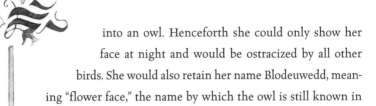

into an owl. Henceforth she could only show her face at night and would be ostracized by all other birds. She would also retain her name Blodeuwedd, meaning "flower face," the name by which the owl is still known in Wales today.

The second, better-known legend connected with the waters is traditional but unrelated to Llew or tales of the *Mabinogion*. It tells of how the young men of Ardudwy were alone with no young women in their district to love. The Vale of Clwyd, in contrast, had more maids than husbands. There had been a long-standing feud between the communities that prevented any courtships, until the young men decided to take matters into their own hands, launching a daring raid to steal away some of the girls while the men of the valley were away travelling. The band made for the mountains of Ffestiniog while messengers recalled the men of the valley. The boys of Ardudwy were greatly outnumbered and yet fought a lengthy, infamous battle until the lake was stained with their blood. The maids despaired as they looked down from on high, for they had come to love their captors, but the carnage continued until only four defenders were left standing. The valley men then closed in, circled, and plied them with spears and stones. A great cry went up from the maidens, who gathered on a sheer precipice of rock. The sight of the broken bodies of their lovers and kinsmen deranged the girls. Like a flock of birds they threw themselves off the ledge and plunged to their deaths in the depths below, leaving only foaming waters and silence in their wake. Not far from the lakeshore lies a great pile of stone which is said to mark the burial place of the men of Ardudwy.

UPRIGHT

Disorientation. Powerful emotions and imagination. Intuition. Empathy. Creativity and sensitivity. Illusion. Wild visions. Mercy. Intense, valuable dreams. A need to control emotions, lest one becomes fascinated by phantasmagoric dreams and flashes from the subconscious. The underworld. Primordial instincts. Powerful mood swings. Hysteria. Memory. Shadows. Shifting shapes. Familiar landscape transformed under the light of the moon. Seeking mysteries. Strange encounters. Personality complexes. Increasing sensitivity to unseen forces. Magnetism. Tides of emotion. Art source. A fertile period, but a need for conscious control over fears and imagination. The light of reason needed to guard against influence and deception.

REVERSED

Lies. Danger near water. Betrayal. Fear. Repression. Poor judgment. Feeling alienated, removed from life. Having to contend with an exhausting, lawless imagination. Paranoia and hysteria. Mental illness. Lunacy.

19: The Sun

DESCRIPTION

The traditional tarot imagery depicts a golden youth riding a pale horse, naked but for a wrap of red fabric. The sun with its warm rays bathes and dominates the scene. A wall is usually seen in the background, giving the impression of a secret garden or protected paradise.

Llew Llaw Gyffes

Beyond his tale in the Mabinogion we have little in the way of stories of Llew Llaw Gyffes, meaning "bright one of the skillful hand." He was said to have grown at twice the rate of a normal child, could manage any horse, and was perfect in feature, stature, and form. Yet we glimpse a broader view of his character in looking to his Irish equivalent in Lug of the Long Arm, who also is skilled with a spear and sling, as well as being multitalented, declaring himself a warrior, bard, magician, healer, cup bearer, etc. As a solar deity, his festival is Lughnasa, celebrated August 1 during the peak growing season when the wheat ripens under the full strength of the sun. He is the warm, masculine consort to the feminine, flowering earth. Tradition credits Lug with invention of the game fidchell, which is likened to chess, and the harvest festival is celebrated with sport and games of reason. As a shining, wholesome hero, some of his attributes are taken on by later heroes such as Lancelot in skill or Gawaine in his waxing and waning solar powers.

As Llew appears in the Mabinogion, he was born to Arianrhod, who disowned the babe with a zealous hatred. She saddled her son with a difficult fate of three barbs (see the Wheel of Fortune card), the last of which prevented him from having a wife of the human race and leads to one of the best-known passages in Welsh mythology . . .

Together the great magicians Gwydion and Math set about to trump the third fate of Arianrhod's curse by conjuring a woman from the stuff of nature to be the wife of Llew. She was made from the water of the ninth wave and blossoms of oak, broom, and meadowsweet, and given the name Blodeuwedd, meaning "flower face." Gwydion gave his nephew the land of Ardudwy and together with his fair bride they ruled wisely; the land prospered and the couple were much loved. All was well until one evening, with Llew away, Blodeuwedd offered lodgings (as was the custom) to a chieftain who hunted nearby. The magicians had not secured her heart, and thus Blodeuwedd and Gronw Pebyr fell deeply in love. Together they plotted the death of Llew, who in being of divine origin could only be harmed under extraordinary circumstances. To learn the requirements for his death, Blodeuwedd deceived Llew into thinking she asked after the details out of concern for his safety. Llew willingly disclosed all: he must be neither inside nor outdoors, one foot must rest upon the belly of a he-goat and the other in a cauldron that has been used as a bath and topped with a thatch roof. The weapon must be a spear wrought only when people attend mass on Sundays.

A year passed and Blodeuwedd set the stage for the crime, with cauldron and all else, asking Llew if he would enact the scene so that she may understand how to guard against such danger. In his loving trust Llew obliged, and Gronw took aim. However, the spear did not kill Llew, who at being wounded gave an unearthly cry and rose into the air in the shape of an eagle, and was gone. With news of the crime, Gwydion began a search for Llew and was eventually led to an oak tree by a sow who fed from rotting flesh and vermin at its foot. The wasting bird high in its branches was a pitiful sight, and with great tenderness Gwydion sang to Llew, coaxing him down to rest in his lap, and then with magic he restored Llew to the shape of a man. In time he healed and then vowed retribution. At word of Gwydion's return, Blodeuwedd and her maidens fled, and the magician pursued them into the mountains, where he transformed Blodeuwedd into the shape of an owl to live out her days (see the Moon card). Llew demanded that he be allowed to return aim of the spear while Gronw, in turn, stood in the very spot Llew had fallen. Before taking his position, Gronw asked if he might shield himself with a stone slab since his crime had been conceived under the influence of love. Llew relented, yet the spear traveled through the stone and killed Gronw. With Llew healed and restored as lord, the land prospered once more, and later expanded to encompass Gwynedd.

UPRIGHT

Triumph, success, and security. Growth, well-being, and nourishment. Solutions, faith, and glory. Sincerity in love. Play, vacation, and enjoying the blessings in life without analysis. Being present in the moment. Rejuvenation. Childlike innocence and playful manner. Youth. Trust. Blossoming. Thriving. Enjoying the pleasures of nature. Bounty after trials. Masculine, sexual energy. Summer love, country romance. Bright, warm days. Learning new skills through play. Thanksgiving. Birth of a child. Fame.

REVERSED

Means much the same, only to a lesser degree: limited progress, short time in the sun. Frivolity, vanity, and susceptibility. Poor sportsmanship. Spoiled, demanding temperament. Play becoming tiresome or to one's detriment.

20: Judgement

DESCRIPTION

The traditional tarot imagery depicts the scene of the Last Judgement, with one or more angelic figures blowing a horn or trumpet dominating the upper half of the card. In the foreground, the earth begins to open and a number of entombed dead, or sleeping saints, rise from their graves or clasp their hands in prayer. The Last Judgement is the accounting event to proceed the last and greatest battle between good and evil.

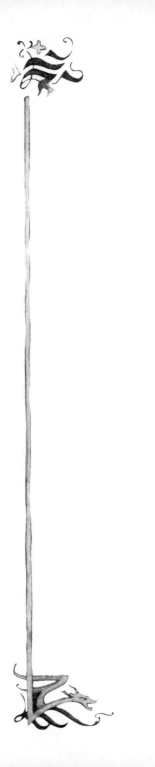

The Sleepers

Wales is rich in Arthurian tradition and one version of Arthur's last days places his battle with Mordred in the shadow of Mount Snowdon. He is said to have fallen in a shower of arrows in the pass that lies between Snowdon and the neighbouring peak of Lliwedd. The knights then carried their king up the ridge and into a cave known as the Cave of Snowdonia's Youths. Legend says that Arthur and his warriors still lie in the cave asleep on their shields until the day when their country is in need of them. The mountain is also known by the name Yr Wyddfa Fawr, meaning "the great tomb," said to refer to the cairn that once stood on its summit.

The "sleepers" are an old theme of legend with numerous heroes awaiting their country's call, such as Charlemagne of France, Brian Boroimhe in Ireland, and Fionn MacCumhail, who is said to sleep in both Ireland and Scotland. A number of locales in Wales claim the cave of Arthurian sleepers, and a second great Welsh hero in Owaine of the Red Hand is said to lie cloaked with his warriors near Carreg Cennen Castle in west Wales. In some tales, a bell hangs in the cave, but older accounts say it is a horn, which, if blown three times, will rouse the warriors. An account collected in northwest Scotland tells of Fionn Mac Cool, lying in a cave together with the warriors known as the Fianna and Fionn's huge hound. Care is taken with the details of the tale, which clarifies that they do not truly sleep, but rather their state is deeply self-absorbed. Having been maintained in oral tradition and then transcribed, the story is told with the evocative refrain: They heard the falling waters,

and storms passed overhead unheeded...Thousands of years
went past (Mackenzie, Teutonic Myth & Legend).

 While some sleepers may be forgotten in our modern times,
the Welsh sleepers are of a strong stock, with their tale being told often and
with varying details and caves. There is a popular version which has
Arthur and his knights sleeping in a cave at the top of the Neath Valley...

A Welsh cowherd was visiting London where a polite but strange man took an interest in his hazel staff. He asked the surly Welshman if he remembered where he had cut the stick, for the hazel marks the spot where great riches are to be found. The cowherd suspected the man to be a magician and took him to the old hazel root which grew in the Neath Valley, where he dug until reaching a flat stone. Prising the stone aside, they entered a narrow passage leading downward to a large cave bathed in a red light. The magician pointed to a bell and warned the cowherd not to touch, lest it all be over for them both. The scene unfolded to reveal the awesome sight of hundreds of warriors asleep on their shields in full battle dress, with swords close at hand and spears planted at their sides. The magician explained the sleepers to be the Pendragon and his knights, who had slept for over a thousand years, awaiting the sound of the bell that would wake them in the country's hour of need, when they would destroy the enemy and restore a king at Caer Lleon. The two quickly helped themselves to the gold that lay on the floor and made ready to leave. But the cowherd so longed to see the knights stir that he could not resist ringing the bell. The ground shook and groaned as the warriors stirred in their steel to rise upon their elbows. A great voice rose from their midst, asking, "Who rang the bell? Has the day come?" The magician shook with fright and called back, "No, the day has not come. Sleep on!" But the great figure did not ease. Again, the magician called out, "The day has not come. It is still night. Sleep on, great Arthur!" The king's voice then came strong and sweet, urging the knights to sleep on, for it was not the day of war between the gold and black eagle, but only thieves who rang the bell. The two then made their escape, after which the entrance and magician vanished, leaving the Welsh man to live out his life in poor health and a futile search for the cave.

The tale told of the Snowdon sleepers is similar if not as fanciful as the preceding story, and therefore likely to be an older root of the mythology. Furthermore, the Snowdon version preserves the early tradition of the intruder being a shepherd who falls in upon the cave while trying to rescue an animal. He accidentally disturbs the sleepers, who lie with hazel wands in their hands. Like the thieves, he is terrified by the rousing warriors and escapes only to live a life of poor health. A German variation of the legend has the intruder reach to steal the robe of a Roman sleeper, only to have his arm wither to a sprout. The detail of the heroes being recalled in aid of their country seems to be a later addition to a very old mythology which stressed sorrow and disaster to follow any disturbance of the dead or "sleeping."

UPRIGHT

Hearing the call to a new life. Resurrection. Rebirth. New perception and purpose in life. A reawakening. Renewed enthusiasm. A rising destiny. Unexplored path. Invitation, recognizing new opportunities. Creating a new philosophy and purpose. Reaching a crossroads and assessing one's past life, motives, values, and progress. Rite of passage. Evaluating one's moral conscience and questioning what one has believed and valued up to this time. A clearing away of dogma, outside expectations, propaganda, and conventional, unquestioned wisdom that has accumulated and entombed one's life. Self-evaluation. Expanding vision and philosophy. Accepting responsibility for self-imposed limitations and how one's actions have affected others. Having the courage to make necessary changes to bring about growth and purpose.

REVERSED

Delusion. Denying the truth of a matter. Chasing rainbows. Being proved wrong. Having misjudged a situation. Remorse and disappointment. Or, depending on surrounding cards, may be lack of faith or unwarranted doubts. Repentance.

21: The Universe

DESCRIPTION

The traditional tarot imagery of the Universe or World card generally depicts a woman dancing, as in "Liberty does a pirouette." She appears nude but for a sash of fabric and gently holds a wand or wands in her hand, symbolic of being in control of her own fate. Sometimes the symbols of the evangelists appear in the four corners of the card as in the man, bull, lion, and eagle.

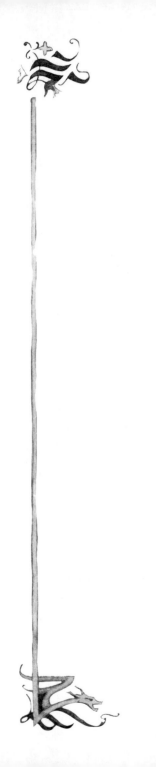

Cadair Idris

The mountain of Cadair Idris in north Wales (*Cadair* meaning "chair") has long been thought of as haunted, and a gathering place for otherworldly characters and forces. Gwyn ap Nudd, lord of the underworld, is said to lead the Wild Hunt through the sky to circle the peak every Halloween. The Wild Hunt is a fantastic sight with the souls of the dead racing upon spectral horses and stags, accompanied by illuminous white hounds with red-tipped ears. The *cwn annwn* (meaning "hounds of the Otherworld") are more often seen without the Wild Hunt, as a pack careening about the slopes of Cadair Idris, where they like to fill the night with eerie, echoing cries. Idris was the name of a historical seventh-century prince who was important in battling the invading Irish. But the name more commonly conjures up the image of the giant Idris, who is said to have liked to stand on the summit of his mountain and throw boulders into distant parts of Wales, thus providing an imaginative explanation for large solitary rocks that came to rest in odd places with the retreat of the Ice Age. Idris had a great passion for star gazing and had a chair carved of living rock on the summit, where he would sit and contemplate the universe. Tradition speaks of a rock on the summit which resembles a chair, and claims if one spends the night on the mountain, they will descend in the morning either a gifted poet or a madman. An even older tradition claims the same power of a hollow beneath a ledge of rock on Mount Snowdon, known as the Black Stone of Arrdu. Likewise, west Wales claims the great prophet and poet Myrddin had a chair on the height of Merlin's Hill, also formed of living rock, where he was said to have delivered his prophecies.

Down through the centuries, bards would meet for the purpose of regulating the profession and staging contests of music and poetry, with the pinnacle of accomplishment being the prize of "the chair." The hierarchy within the bardic world placed the title of "chief of song" upon its highest rank of poet, who would occupy a distinguished seat at the royal court. The practice of "chairing" the winning poet echoes this custom, while gatherings themselves are known as an eisteddfod, deriving from the word *eistedd*, "to sit." It is assumed such events have been held from earliest times, yet the oldest surviving record of an eisteddfod dates from 1176, and they continue today as the National Eisteddfod, which has been an annual event since 1881. The National Eisteddfod has been of value to Welsh literature in promoting the art and bringing recognition to its participants, and yet there remains the uneasy relationship in pairing competition and art.

In the distant past, the poetic gift of the bard was considered supernatural and closely associated with the prophecy. The bards themselves played upon this idea, provoking awe in the peasantry and cultivating wary respect among the nobility. Even today we tend to think of two differing approaches to art, the one being psychological, the other visionary. The psychological art draws from one's own life in characters, environment, and drama, to resonate with the populace as common experience. The visionary art, on the other hand, is far beyond the experience of the individual artist, who becomes a mere portal for glimpses of sublime, unfathomable mysteries of the beyond, which we may sense in art and yet not gaze upon directly. Carl Jung, in his essay "Psychology and Literature," described the realm of the visionary artist as the primordial abyss—"pregnant with meaning, yet chilling the blood with strangeness" (Jung, *The Spirit in Man, Art, and Literature*). The very potency of visionary art can make it repellant to some, and a little dangerous to the artist, who manifests the art through ecstasy, as the Welsh described the state. Neurotic behaviour and genius carry many of the same symptoms, hence the warning in the tradition of Cadair Idris of descending from its peak inspired or mad.

The twelfth-century writings of Giraldus Cambrensis speak of a particular class of seer-poet known as *awenyddion*, or "inspired people." The poets would place themselves in a trance-like state and when consulted would roar out the prophecy, most of which was unintelligible, but on closer examination provided an answer in one word or sentence, appearing within the poetic flourishings. The prophecies of the awenyddion, whether accurate or not, provided a sense of security and destined purpose in times of upheaval. Their words could rally and restore order to a population which had begun to fragment under stress. It was within their power to chart a new course in uncertain times, and so, too, they could be seen as a tool of propaganda.

In some ways the isolation and communion sought on the summit of Cadair Idris resembles the vision quest of the North American Indian, and yet there is a marked difference in that the vision quest seeks guidance as to the personal path and the Celtic bard on Cadair Idris seeks art in a place of mystery or memory that is meant to ascend this plane and speak to the world at large. In attaining the broader vision, the poet's role resembles that of the shaman in serving the community as a whole. The bard was accustomed to think outside himself in writing his poetry, by "becoming," for example, a historical figure or witness to an event, thereby making his composing an esoteric art. It is awesome to think on such powerful imaginations opening to the night sky atop a windswept Cadair Idris.

UPRIGHT

Ascension. Opening to a higher dimension. Culmination and synthesis. Enlightenment. Attaining a broader view of life. Moving beyond the personal to become aware of the interconnected nature of life. Harmony and perfection. Peace and freedom of thought. Inspiration and comprehension. Ecstasy. Glimpses, however brief, of the great mysteries of life. Being able to appreciate the larger scene or patterns in life. Faith. Epiphany. A heightened sense of being alive. Purpose. Confidence. Completion. Enjoying life and anticipating its curves. Unencumbered by the trivial. Being in control of one's fate. Intelligence. Independence. Determination and stability. Strength and enthusiasm. Intuition and spiritual heights. Crowning achievement. Reward and promotion. Graduation. Lasting happiness. As the last of the major arcana, the Universe represents the height of a progression. The Universe card is associated with the four evangelists, Matthew, Luke, Mark, and John, who in turn are equated with incarnation, passion, resurrection, and ascension, respectively.

REVERSED

Having lost or being unable to maintain one's centre. Lack of nourishment and support. Spiritual starvation. Enslavement or control. Scattered energies. Insurmountable obstacles. Sacrifice. Blockage. Arrested development.

The · Minor ·
Arcana

Suit of Wands

Wands symbolize the power of the intellect and intuitive thinking. They represent accomplishment and success in the full sense of an evolved person or purpose which contributes to the community at large. Wands signify valuing more than money, and advancing and enhancing quality of life, whether by arts, sciences, humanitarian causes, etc. Other keywords include self-reliance, initiative, self-made persons, visionary art, ideals, conviction, and wisdom.

Ace of Wands

Inspiration. Rising to a challenge. Breakthrough in thinking. Self-reliance, spiritual strength, and confidence. Conviction and faith in vision or path. Reason reigning over impulse. Ideas empowered by desire. Creative heights and achievement. Quick thinking, humour, and balance. Revelations and transcendent thoughts. Fruitful plans and far-reaching ideas. Empathy and understanding. Marriage and fertility.

REVERSED

Lack of enthusiasm. Arrested development. The limits of conventional thinking. Oppression. Lack of experience. Apathy. Spiritual malnutrition.

Two of Wands

Planning. Using one's intuition to search out new possibilities and hidden options. Foresight. Viewing a situation from a higher perspective. Brainstorming and consideration. Weighing of options. Using one's imagination. Anticipating obstacles and uncertainty. Assessing one's own capabilities. Focus and executive responsibilities.

REVERSED

A creative block. Being ill-prepared for the task at hand. Avoiding responsibility. Dread, pessimism, and delays. Thwarted plans and loss.

Three of Wands

Speculation. Launching of a new enterprise. Investigating new directions. Exploring adventure. Distributing energy and resources. A gamble on the unknown. Diversifying. Optimism. Expansion. Broadening horizons. Taking the initiative. Trade and negotiations. Research. Educated decisions.

REVERSED

Difficulty getting a venture off the ground. Painful first steps. Premature attempt. Learning experience. Need for calm discipline, research, and thorough planning.

Four of Wands

Repose after difficulty. A prize. Unexpected celebration. Social events. Romance and fertility. Virtue, vigilance, and restraint are rewarded. Tide turned in one's favour. Solid foundation for the future. Alliances and friendship. Sharing. Relief. On a deeper level, the card represents equilibrium and achieving a state of balance, peace, and contentment after a long ordeal. Gratitude. Emotional and psychological well-being.

REVERSED

Small, irritating setbacks. Stubborn snags. Lack of outside interest. Progress, but time and effort could be better spent elsewhere. Being caught in a behavioural rut. Sarcasm.

Five of Wands

Competition. Erratic energy. Confusion. Inconsistent effort. Preoccupation with material acquisitions. Appearing a fool in trying to keep up with the Joneses. Overspending. Impatience and stress. Waxing and waning of purpose. Clash of ideas and principles. Sloppy effort. Rebellion and turmoil. Breakdown of communication. Hurting others by giving mixed messages. Need to reevaluate situation, organize, and start afresh.

REVERSED

Arguments. Trickery. Contradictions. Reaching a dead end. Trespassers. Imposters. Being easily deterred. Faint-hearted hero or heroine.

Six of Wands

Acknowledgement of accomplishments. Victory parade. Accolades, admirers, and gratitude. Respect of one's peers. Contributing ideas to a group project or cause. Leadership and established reputation. Good standing. Recognized authority. Having the confidence of the community. A success being more than one had hoped for. A sense of satisfaction. An original, daring thought brings victory. Honours.

REVERSED

Inconclusive results. Setbacks. Low morale. Wasted time. Unfocused attempt. No clear designated target. Poor showing. Lack of recognition.

Seven of Wands

Courage, determination, and creative thinking. Portends a good time to hazard a gamble. Though the odds may seem against you, there are advantages to your position. The victory of a major battle paves the way to opportunity and a positive cycle in life. Taking a stand. Guarding principles and dreams. Fending off predators. Silencing naysayers.

REVERSED

Danger in doing nothing. A warning to take action of any sort, whether confronting, negotiating, or issuing a challenge. Denying or ignoring a situation only brings future grief. Take a stand.

Eight of Wands

Opportunity. Swift response. Thinking on one's feet. Opening. Adventure. Chance to make great progress if one has the courage and wits to act quickly. Travel entailing a spiritual lesson. Can signify falling in love. Time of hope. Make your move. Opportunity afoot; make haste. Whirlwind of romance. Arrows of love.

REVERSED

Change of heart. Remorse. Quarrels amidst partners and friends. Pangs of conscience. Cost of being unprepared. Choosing to let an opportunity or love die. Fear someone or something too hard to handle or a price too high to pay.

Nine of Wands

Order and control. Planning and preparations. Experience. Guarding one's assets, whether they be ideas for the future or gains made in the past. Anticipating hostility. Reviewing defences. The discipline of a seasoned warrior. Wisdom that has come at a high price. Growth and the refining of one's character through a perilous passage. Preparing for a storm. Deterring or outwitting an adversary.

REVERSED

Calamity. Failed defences. Time of adversity. Failure to foresee consequences. Unheeded warnings. Being caught off guard.

Ten of Wands

Burden. Rising to a challenge. Not flinching in the face of hard work. Pressure. Effort and time. Asserting oneself. Oppression followed by gain. Sustaining others. Carrying one's weight and more. Saving for a home. Budget restrictions. Perseverance. Suppressing one's needs to accomplish a demanding task.

REVERSED

Being foiled by a perceived shortcut. Being duped. Being distracted by glitter. Succumbing to intrigues. Being led astray. Shirking responsibilities. Shallow, self-serving philosophy.

Page of Wands

Arrival of a positive phase. Good news brought by a cheerful friend or ally. Youth, potential, and flexibility. Socializing. Being open to new ideas. Stimulation. Broadening horizons. A true, faithful heart. Play and excitement.

REVERSED

Instability. A worrisome child. Gossip and insincerity. A loose tongue. Immaturity. Lack of communication. Gullibility due to lack of experience or knowledge.

Knight of Wands

A quick, clever man with a sense of humour. One with an unusual way of looking at life, recognizing patterns and opportunities missed by others. He is somewhat unpredictable, making for stimulating company. A man who inspires with his enthusiasm and gift of language. A considerate and loyal person. A journey or change of residence. Sound instincts.

REVERSED

Irreconcilable differences. A heated exchange. Loss of relationship. A man who sows strife for amusement. Weak ideas.

Queen of Wands

An intelligent woman with a warm heart. She is admired for being self-made, having earned her standing in the world by way of her own hard work and talents. This experience makes her sensitive to the struggles of others she finds worthy. Courage, conviction, high ideals. A steadfast supporter. A woman who stimulates and teaches those around her. A person of intellectual influence. Politics and education. While she enjoys luxury, she values accomplishment and attempts to leave her mark on society.

REVERSED

A strident, sharp-tongued woman. Unpleasant company. Anger causing one to become judgmental and habitually suspicious. Unsympathetic, alienating behaviour.

King of Wands

Status, honour. An intellectual, artistic force who is more stable than the Knight of Wands. A man who has succeeded due to his own intelligence and determination. Overcoming a disadvantaged start in life to reach a position of influence and satisfaction. The card represents more than the material success which may accompany his rise—it is achievement that contributes to the arts, sciences, or quality of life. A life well lived.

REVERSED

A bore. One with an inflated sense of self-importance who takes little trouble over others. A man who cannot recognize achievement beyond material success.

Suit of
Swords

Swords represent action. They are the impetus to impact and interact with the world around us. Bravery, leadership, and responsibility are symbolized by swords. Whether the passionate force is unleashed for good or ill depends on the governing mind; hence, destruction and danger can also be represented by the suit.

Ace of Swords

Action. Great, rising force. Taking control. Determination. Energy. Swiftness. Bringing about change. Direction and enacting ideas. Quick, clever, decisive action. Implementing plans. Follow through. Release of energy and pressure. Confidence. Conviction. Heroics and focus. Discriminating powers—cutting through and free of the briar. Cutting ties. Clearing the air. Sense of timing. Harnessing the winds. Rocking the boat. Engaging life.

REVERSED

Premature use of force. Excessive force resulting in chaos and violence. All passion spent. Quick temper. Overweening desires. Goals at any price.

Two of Swords

Armed peace. Uncertainty. Limited information. Impasse. Blind judgment. Sensing. Frail alliance but with potential. Invitation to friendship, collaboration, or union, but not being met halfway. Questioning whether friend or foe. Dual nature. Energized by a not yet decided situation, relationship, or path venturing into the unknown. Having to proceed while in the dark, using intuition or caution. Self-reliance. Having to make a blind choice to break a stalemate.

REVERSED

Encountering lies and deceit. Being let down. Having to accept that you misjudged a person or situation. Cowardice in others.

Three of Swords

Heartache. Hurt. Harsh resolution. Distress. Having been abandoned. Severance. Feeling crippled by the weight of past hurts. The pain of being misunderstood or unfairly judged. Rejection. Estrangement. Fear and isolation. Separation. The pain of a triangle dynamic in relationship or interests. The need for mental control over emotions. Frail health.

REVERSED

Lingering conflict. Difficulty healing. A long, challenging journey to recovery. A persistent, unrequited love. Unhealthy involvements and associations. Breakdown. Bewilderment.

Four of Swords

Reprieve. Vigil. Withdrawal and silence. Waiting. Isolation and asylum. Existence taking on a surreal feeling, as if one is veiled from life. A seemingly deathlike sleep phase in life, but a time which incubates future dreams. Exile. A freeze on life protecting one from injury or self-destructive behaviour. Recovery. Convalescence. Keeping hidden. Protection in silence. Possibly being forsaken. Warning that a quest may be endangering one's health. Need for help from others. Hospital stay or finding sanctuary.

REVERSED

Prison. Excessively strict environment. Exile and depression. Abandonment. Exhaustion caused by battling overwhelming odds over an extended time. Fruitless struggle.

Five of Swords

Loss, sorrow, regret. Defeat. Overwhelming opposition. Thwarted by obstacles. Loss of confidence. Sometimes being made to suffer the sins of others. Lack of strength and resources. Feeling disoriented. Loss of blood. Misjudging a situation or person. Rash action. Humiliation. Unfortunate meeting. Mercy or the lack of it.

REVERSED

Excessive force. Gossip and slander. A malicious person or group. A threatening situation. Ambush, sabotage. Need for caution. Protection in numbers.

Six of Swords

Movement. Improvement of any situation. Safe passage. More than sympathy, but help from others. Moving away from an unhealthy situation. Lessening stress, yet destination unknown. Travel over water. A new chapter. Sometimes interpreted as a declaration of love. Direction. A powerful card in aligning heart and mind. Focus and follow-through, yet unpredictable result.

REVERSED

Confession. Explanation. Surprise. Anxiety. Delay of travel. An unpleasant atmosphere. Harassment. Frustration.

Seven of Swords

Resignation. Acceptance. Limited success. Releasing of the old renews the spirit. Rejecting outside expectations for an individually fashioned lifestyle. End of an ordeal. Negotiations. Independent thinking. Confidence. Release from the grip of material questing for higher pursuits.

REVERSED

Debasing of talents. Warning. Instruction. Having to contend with uneducated critics. Discouragement. Narrow views. A lack of support or understanding.

Eight of Swords

Frustration and fear. Feeling powerless and at the mercy of outside forces. The controlling behaviour of others. Unfair treatment. A pawn. Not having the ability to adequately protect oneself. Vulnerable to deceit. Scapegoat. Pleas falling on deaf ears. Being misunderstood. Being used. A temporary situation that will pass.

REVERSED

Betrayal. Unexpected aggression. Threatening situation. Can represent illness. The need to be on guard.

Nine of Swords

Nightmares, suspicion, and insecurity. Depression weighing one down. Worry and delays. Longing and misery. Pining for a loved one. Distress and obsession. The haunting of past hurts and injustices. Debilitating, unhealthy situation. Unrelenting enemy. Loneliness. Indecision. Bewilderment. Premature end.

REVERSED
Shame. An imposter. A state of denial. Unrequited love. Cruel gossip.

Ten of Swords

Conflict. Destruction. Loss. Breakdown of relationships. Slander. Hurt. Misfortune. Plans that seemed promising end in failure. Disillusion. Grief. Temporary alliances. Being forsaken. A sacrifice. Withdrawing from the world due to trauma. The apex and end of a matter. Does not represent violent death.

REVERSED

Short-term gains. Fallacy. Merger gain. Overconfidence. Poor research. Brief respite. Mirage. Gullibility.

Page of Swords

Secrets. Hidden matters. Need for caution. Plots. Sensing under-current of dangers afoot. Being privy to confidential matters. Being given inside information and warnings. Spies. A slippery adversary. Infected environment. A philosophy that sanctions unfair practices so long as serving one's purpose. Enquiring mind finds lies. Reason to be suspect.

REVERSED

Exposure. Matter brought to light. Depending on surrounding cards, may mean freedom and relief at being left or caught. A confidence betrayed.

Knight of Swords

Daring, impressive young man of action. An impulsive but usually well-meaning person. Heroic, if a little rash. A man who can be wearing and disruptive, but also effective. Being determined, intelligent, and single-minded. Goals taking priority over relationships. A mercenary. Standing up for oneself or others. Bringing matters to a head.

REVERSED

A man who revels in conflict. A bitter person who resents the happiness of others. Disrespect of women. An inadequate, jealous chauvinist or bigot.

Queen of Swords

An impressive, empowering, trailblazing woman. Courage and intelligence. Steely determination. Revolutionary, pioneering qualities. Confidence. One who will not be held down by convention. Even if she appears mild-mannered, at her core she remains an independent, even rebellious spirit. Gains. Taking control. No-nonsense sort of woman. May be careless or unsympathetic with the feelings of others.

REVERSED

Overweening ambition. Greed and lust for power. Dangerous, even violent woman. Fanatical zeal. Abuse. Jealousy.

King of Swords

A powerful man with a quick temper. He is no fool and should be handled with care. A daring, impressive, effective leader, if a little harsh. A man of influence and long reach. Tenacity. Passion and conviction. An authority. Commanding presence. Impact, bravery, and ambition.

REVERSED

A merciless opponent. Extremes. An unbalanced, dangerous man. Misuse of power. Corruption. Prejudice, bigotry, and disrespect. An unscrupulous man who believes himself untouchable and entitled to his appetites. Abomination and decay.

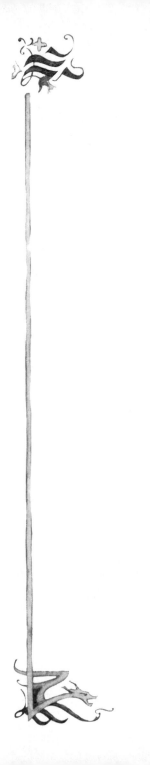

Suit of
Cups

Cups represent the emotions, creativity, and the soulful aspects of life. Visionary art, devotion, charity, and protection are among the more demanding aspects of the suit, which also includes the gentle influences of goodwill, friendship, and empathy. Cups are symbolic of the life force as fertility, nourishment, and nurture. Desire, attraction, love, and union belong to the suit as a powerful brew of nature's cauldron.

Ace of Cups

Joy, well-being, nourishment, and beauty. Fertility, creation, and devotion. Protection. The beginning of a blessed, fruitful phase in life. May refer to a cause, project, or idea with soul. The card of true love. Marriage of equals which is of benefit to those people close to the couple or their cause. A force for good. Consummated union. The well of love, art, devotion, and compassion. Divine inspiration and protection. Brave heart. A great love that even if unrequited or thwarted still bestows the creative and transformative power, heights, and knowledge that otherwise would remain unknown.

REVERSED

Rejection. Fear and confusion. Loss of faith. Being forsaken. Injury, grief, and resignation. Death of love. Emptiness and despair. Sacrifice.

Two of Cups

Romance, love, attraction of opposites. Union. Magnetism. Dance of courtship. Entwining energies. Sparks. The flow and grace of a natural match. Forming emotional bonds. Sharing, stability in give and take. Balanced ebb and flow of emotions. Curiosity, affection, and excitement. Most often symbolizes a romantic partnership, but may refer to a friendship or alliance with an emotional component and compatibility of a kindred polarity. Engagement or marriage.

REVERSED

Cowardice. False love and weakness. Jealousy. Outside influences damage the fragile growth of a new relationship. The intense energy of a good match gone awry proves equally passionate in the negative direction. Panic, hurt, sabotage.

Three of Cups

Celebration. Thanksgiving. Shared happiness. Pleasure and satisfaction. Enrichment of friendships. Support, encouragement. Excitement and play. Enjoying arts and talents. Luck, excitement, and momentum. Goodwill and humour. The doubling effect of success shared. The joy of artistic collaboration. Romantic fun. The freshness of spring. Gratitude and good health.

REVERSED

Remains a positive card, but indicates material pleasures with a less emotional component. Small gains. Wasting resources. Exploiting the environment or kindness of people.

Four of Cups

Discontent and isolation. Feeling at a loss as to what can be done to improve a situation. Doubt. Melancholy. A disenchanting experience. Disgust. Can also indicate being fussy. Having to deal with naysayers. Not recognizing what one has. It is an encouraging card, indicating help that seems to be divine intervention ensuring one has all the cups one needs.

REVERSED

Suspicion. Blaming others for one's situation. Playing on the undeserved sympathy of others. Insecurity.

Five of Cups

Disappointment. Being held at a disadvantage and manipulated by emotional strings. Unfulfilled dreams. Feeling an energy drain. Spilled milk. Suffering over one's suffering. Difficulty accepting a loss. Disbelief. Senseless loss. Lingering gloom. Being limited by the haunting of past experience. Weight. Slow healing.

REVERSED

Bitterness. An unhappy marriage. Unfulfilled expectations. Regret. Sad news. Poor choice of alliance. Reunion with an old lover. Need to guard against self-delusion. Inheritance.

Six of Cups

Friendship. Play. Remembering past happiness and childlike innocence. Renewal. Nostalgia. Pleasant company. Reminiscing with old friends. Drawing strength from shared experiences. Being understood and appreciated. Teamwork. Taking pleasure in simple, wholesome activities and surroundings. Seeing the good in life.

REVERSED

Change of scenery and connections. New stage. Separation from old friends. Losing touch with the past. A natural progression and passing.

Seven of Cups

Dreams. A fertile imagination. Numerous and sometimes con-
flicting desires. Dreaming up options. Window shopping for
paths and goals. Fertility in mind and spirit. Bemused and confused by the possibilities of options. Unexpected turn of events.
Realization of a long shot. Surprises. Triumph of the underdog.
Humour, thrills, and vision.

REVERSED

Extreme effects of alcohol or drug abuse. Clouded judgment.
Being ruled by emotion. Exaggerated daydreams or nightmares.
Mercy. Creative heights. Channeling passions.

Eight of Cups

Turning away. Giving up. Finding that something or someone was not a healthy influence. River run dry. Choosing to sacrifice in order to make a clean break and start afresh elsewhere. Abandoning a dream. Changing directions. The dawn of something new. A quest with heart. Bravery. Heeding the call.

REVERSED

A timid nature attracts predators. Unhealthy situation being drawn out over time. Denying the negative impact of a relationship. Taboos.

Nine of Cups

Fertile surroundings. Nourishment. Natural beauty. Delight. Romance. Summer's cauldron of all good things for the heart. Relief and well-being. Blossoming. Seduction and pleasures. Gentle, inspiring surroundings and company. Warm, encouraging atmosphere. Luck. The feel of enchanted evenings.

REVERSED

Limited potential and success. Small setbacks. Relationship not carrying the nutrient and stimulus hoped for. Too much in common, whereas diversity brings strength and enrichment.

Ten of Cups

Full heart. Blessings. Higher, mature love. True love. Real companionship. Dreams come true. Safety, security, and satisfaction. A giving relationship. Natural order. Home providing joy. Thanksgiving. Trust. A feeling of arrival and freedom. Fruitful partnership. Deep connection. Joining of talents make for a powerful, creative force. Fortunate, natural pairing. Harmony. A dreamy partnership as a source of light and benefit to others.

REVERSED

Outmoded path. Not receiving reward for effort. Indignation. Not being appreciated or understood. Strife and pettiness mar home life. Emotional exhaustion.

Page of Cups

Good news. Invitation. A cheerful young person with a trusting heart. Optimism. Romantic interest. Imagination. Playfulness. Artistic abilities. Compassion and understanding. Birth of a child. An accommodating, well-mannered soul.

REVERSED

Neglect. Oppression of talent. Begrudging and excluding others. Falsehood. Flattery and seduction. One masquerading as an artist.

Knight of Cups

A romantic man. A considerate, creative, artistic sort. Musician, poet, diplomat. A promising proposal or collaboration. An opportunity to learn via a friend or lover. Broadening horizons. New philosophies. Gifts and romance. Loyalty. Sound, romantic advice. Imagination and empathy. Marriage proposal. Reciprocated love. Traditionally the messenger of true love.

REVERSED

An egotist. One so taken with himself that he can speak of little else but his own pursuits. Poor company. A romantic rival who uses gossip to kill love.

Queen of Cups

A woman of imagination. Romantic, compassionate air. One who encourages the dreams and talents of others. Generosity and care. A loyal lover. A genuine heart. Virtue. Protection. A cultured, refined woman who is wise in matters of the heart. For a male querent she can represent true love; for a woman a romantic confidant or rival. Even as rival she is just and honest, believing in fair play.

REVERSED

Perversity. Dishonour. Falsehood and games. A showoff. An imposter. An overly confident actress. A drama queen. A spoiled woman who whines and enjoys the sound of her own voice. Pretension.

King of Cups

A visionary man. A strong, dignified man with a gentle manner who enriches the lives of those around him. An authority. Meaningful accomplishment. Intelligence and influence. Significant artistic abilities. Trust. Ethics. Strength of conviction. Higher principles and higher love. Intuition and foresight. A magnetic, somewhat reclusive, reflective nature.

REVERSED

Self-serving man. One who feeds on the energy of the young that surround him, but gives little in return. Envy. Terroritorial, defensive behaviour. Scandal. Illness.

Suit of
Pentacles

Pentacles represent the practical side of life: business, labour, material goods. Skills and talents that are inherent assets are also symbolized, as well as countable, bankable assets. Pentacles are of the earthly plane, signifying security and sustenance, banking, bookkeeping, commerce, and enterprise. Prosperity and protection as well as the canny, sly business mind are also seen in the suit.

Ace of Pentacles

Gain. Attainment. Increased income. A timely windfall. The beginning of a large project. Recognition of achievements. Treasures. Good, sound foundation to launch an idea. Investors. Both material and emotional well-being. Confidence. Measured excitement. Blessings. Seemingly divine intervention. Relief.

REVERSED

The ill side of wealth—greed, a derelict heart, and ill treatment of others. Jealousy and decay. Abomination of values. The twisting and distorting effects of greed. The narrow, base belief of money being success.

Two of Pentacles

Fluctuating economic fortune. Balancing act. Tricky launch of a new project. Qualms. Risky venture. Timing and dexterity. Shadowy scene and cunning characters. Juggling resources. Thinking on your feet. Agility needed to sail high seas. Uncanny instinct. Crafty business partner. A vague, even peculiar situation that keeps one guessing and on their toes. The dance of opposites. Ambiguity.

REVERSED

Embarrassment. Unheeded warnings. Oversight. Poor research. Ignoring details. Not being suited to the task. Collapse of a project.

Three of Pentacles

Skill. Craft. Making use of talents. Marketable skill or idea. An inherent ability that is a great asset of more than mere monetary value. Being able to take interest and pride in humble work. Finding comfort and peace in one's work. Steady, sure progress. Earning a reputation for quality, though not recognizing your own worth. Maturity and pleasant work environment.

REVERSED

A drain of one's potential. Being cheated of a reward. Losing interest in a task. A need to reconnect or consider an alternative vocation. Lingering doubts. Avoiding work. Poor-quality work.

Four of Pentacles

Guarding one's gains, whether they be possessions, property, or ideas. Overidentifying with one's material wealth. Recalling resources. Closing accounts. Expanding in new directions closer to home or personal interests. Acquiring new possessions. Parading wealth. Danger of ostentation.

REVERSED

Small gain or gift. Modest ambition. Fussing and fretting over tiny details breeds resentment in the workplace. Overwork and worry. Need to delegate tasks.

Five of Pentacles

Loss and wandering. Drained resources. Destitution. Exhaustion. Struggling to stay afloat while searching for relief. Fighting to keep morale and energy levels up. Loneliness. Crossing a wasteland. The collapse of one's values leads to the search for spiritual guidance. Temporary hardship. Seeking refuge.

REVERSED

Creating troubles. Making matters worse. Waste. A money pit. Refusing to accept failure prolongs suffering and prevents aid.

Six of Pentacles

Sharing good fortune. The resolution to a problem. Receiving help, such as a timely commission. Charitable acts. Relief. The settling of a debt. Exchange. Entitlement. Rewarding someone for their effort. Supporting a cause or talent you admire. Balancing the scales. Restitution. Giving credit where deserved.

REVERSED

Jealousy. Exploitation. Envy and worry. The weight of accumulating debts. Being cheated. Theft and greed. Past failures undermining confidence.

Seven of Pentacles

Bounty comes of patience and ingenuity. The fair and just treatment of others. Growth in personal and business life. Feeling of well-being. Satisfaction in work. Profit. A card of goodwill. The repaying of past kindness. Stability and steady progress. Reaping what has been sowed.

REVERSED

Unwise loan or expense. A gamble gone wrong. Alarm. Impatience. Strong competition. Loss of promotion. Miscalculation. Poor luck. Neglect of a project.

Eight of Pentacles

Employment. Commissions. Schedules and deadlines. Focus.
Creative work. Skills and talents put to good use. Knowledge
and experience. A large project or business running as a well-
oiled machine. Maturity of business. Accommodation.
Achievement. Success. Income. Finding one's niche in life.

REVERSED

Loathing the workplace. Avoiding making a choice of career
or lack of ambition. One who manipulates and exploits to
acquire rather than labours. Double standards within a family-
run business. Freeloader. Attitude of a spoiled child.

Nine of Pentacles

Prudence. Assessment. Tallying. Successful handling of a multi-faceted venture. Having speculated and been proven right. Planning and diplomacy. Care in choosing friends and confidants. Compassion, patience, and effort to understand others. Foresight and honourable behaviour. Popularity.

REVERSED

Roguery. Taking advantage of trust. Using others to boost one's self-esteem. Broken promises. Public humiliation at the hands of a cad, social climber, or opportunist.

Ten of Pentacles

Freedom from financial concerns. Prosperity. Strong, established family setting. Protection and stability within a clan. Family traditions and gatherings. Having the time to enjoy the fruits of one's labour. Achieving of worldly dreams. Benefiting from the work of one's predecessors. Gifts, inheritance, archives. Celebrations and reunions.

REVERSED

Gambling, loss, theft. Fickle luck. Fatality. Family conflict. Loss or being cheated out of inheritance. Smeared reputation. Hazardous adventure.

Page of Pentacles

Proposal. Business communications. Offers of exchange. An enthusiastic young person eager to enter the world of commerce. Good ideas. Young achiever. Reliable, hard worker. Discipline. Focus. Questions. Serious student. Good report. Business sense.

REVERSED

Stalled communications. Impasse in negotiations. Misunderstanding. One who spends so much time on work or studies that social skills suffer from arrested development.

Knight of Pentacles

Hardworking young man with a traditional, orthodox outlook.
Utility. An honest, responsible person. Solid progress. Method-
ical approach to large goals. Financial consultant. Commitment, perseverance, and stamina. A dependable man, if considered a little dull.

REVERSED

Unemployment and discouragement. Stagnation. A shallow,
material person. One who can only judge success in terms of
money and cannot comprehend accomplishment on its own
merit. A bore. Spoiled offspring. Laziness.

Queen of Pentacles

A capable business woman. Calm, steady progress under the leadership of a woman. Security. A woman of substance and earthy nature. A strong role model who supports and protects those around her. A caring, fair employer. An investor. A careful manager. An intelligent, prudent, wealthy woman.

REVERSED

A controlling woman. A bully. One who cares little for anything but money. Overweening greed. Abuse of the vulnerable. A calculating sort who befriends only to serve her own ends. Suspicion, danger. Beware of one lacking a conscience.

King of Pentacles

A proud, self-assured man. Established wealth. Security and social status. A grounded, practical leader. An intelligent man who, if not talented himself, values and supports the gifts of others. Recognizing the value of culture to a society. Money with ethical conscience. Practical help and skills. A supportive husband.

R E V E R S E D

Corruption. Self-centered old man. Dangerous, unethical enemy. Perversity and vice. Material, unfaithful man. Employee unrest.

Glossary

Afagddu: son of Ceridwen, representing darkness.

Amangons: a king who was known to rape and steal from virgin guardians of wells before the Arthurian age.

Ambrosius: brother to Uther Pendragon in the Arthurian legend.

Aneirin: late sixth-century Welsh poet to whom the epic poem Y *Gododdin* is attributed.

Annwn: "otherworld" or "underworld"; a land of the dead or ancestors but not to be confused with hell.

Arawn: lord of Annwn, or "otherworld."

Arderydd: a battlefield where Myrddin (Merlin) went mad.

Ardudwy: the home lands of Llew Llaw Gyffes.

Arianrhod: mother of Llew Llaw Gyffes and Dylan. Sister of Gywdion.

Awen: "inspiration" or "muse."

Awenyddion: "inspired people"; class of seer-bard.

Badger in the Bag: a "game" of beating a man in a bag, as in the fate of Rhiannon's suitor Gwawl.

Bard: educated poet and musician.

Bardd teulu: "poet of the retinue."

Black Knight: the guardian of a miraculous fountain and champion of the Lady of the Fountain.

Black Stone of Arrdu: a ledge on Mount Snowdon said to bestow the gift of poetry if a person were to spend the night beneath the stone.

Blodeuwedd: "flower face"; the bride created from flowers by Gwydion and Math for Llew Llaw Gyffes, who was barred from marrying a woman of the human race.

Bran the Blessed: the much-loved king and giant brother of Branwen.

Branwen: sister to Bran the Blessed. Tradition names her as one of the ancestresses of Britain.

Breton: as deriving from Brittany of N.W. France.

Brittany: region of N.W. France.

Cadair Idris: name of Welsh mountain meaning "chair of Idris."

Cantre'r Gwaelod: "bottom hundred"; the name for the kingdom said to lie submerged under the waters of Cardigan Bay.

Cardigan Bay: waters off the mid- to northwest coast of Wales.

Cerddorion: in Latin, "joculators."

Ceridwen: goddess or witch whose cauldron bestows inspiration and knowledge.

Cernunnos: a name for the pagan Horned God or God of the Hunt.

Cornwall: county in the southwest of England.

Creiddylad: a maid thought to represent the land in the rivalry between Gwyn ap Nudd and Gwythyr ap Greidawl, who fight for her hand every May first.

Creirwy: daughter of Ceridwen, representing beauty and light.

Custennin: a giant shepherd or wild herdsman appearing in the tale of Kilhwch and Olwen.

Cwn annwn: "hounds of the Otherworld" who accompany the Wild Hunt and Arawn.

Dahud: the pagan daughter of Gradlon, who gave her the prosperous city of Kers-Ys, which was swallowed by the sea.

Dylan Eil Ton: "son of the wave"; brother of Llew Llaw Gyffes.

Dylan Thomas (1914–53): influential modern Welsh poet.

Ecca, King: father of Libane, who neglected a well that then drowned her father's kingdom.

Efnisien: "not peaceful"; half brother of Branwen and Bran.

Eisteddfod: a meeting of bards for the purpose of presenting and promoting poetry and music by way of competition.

Elen: wife of Macsen Wledig, sometimes known as Helen of the Hosts.

Elphin: young man who saves the baby Taliesin from the weir.

Evrawc: father of Peredur.

Ffestiniog: a territory; "land of Ffestin" or "a defensive position."

Fidchell: a game likened to chess and said to be invented by the Irish god Lug of the Long Arm.

Fili: "one who sees"; the Irish class of seer-poet.

Fionn Mac Cool: (known under numerous spellings of the name) the heroic leader of the warriors called the Fianna and a well-known legendary figure shared by the Irish and Scots.

Fisher King: a Grail guardian in the Arthurian tradition.

Gaul: ancient country comprised of lands that are now France, Belgium, the Netherlands, Switzerland, and Germany.

Geoffrey of Monmouth(c. 1100–c. 1155): an influential chronicler who drew on Welsh oral tradition. A Welsh cleric and author of *Prophetiae Merlini*, *Historia Regum Britanniae*, and *Vita Merlini*.

Gilfaethwy: brother of Gwydion; raped Goewin, Math's virgin foot-holder.

Goewin: virgin foot-holder in service of Math.

Gradlon: the father of Dahud who converted to Christianity, narrowly escaped the inundation of Kers-Ys, and left his pagan daughter to drown.

Gronw Pebyr: lover of Blodeuwedd, wife of Llew.

Gwales: island off the southern coast of Wales.

Gwawl: a suitor of Rhiannon and rival of Pwyll.

Gwern: son of Branwen and Matholwch.

Gwion Bach: name of Taliesin in his first life tending the cauldron belonging to Ceridwen.

Gwrhyr: bard with gift for shapeshifting and languages.

Gwyddbwyll: a board game likened to chess.

Gwydion: "scientist magician"; famed, powerful magician and nephew of Math.

Gwyn ap Nudd: a lord of the Otherworld who is said to lead the Wild Hunt to collect the souls of the dead.

Gwynedd: the land of north Wales.

Gwythyr ap Greidawl: a figure thought to represent spring or summer, and rival of Gwyn ap Nudd representing the dark months.

Hafgan: a king of Annwn and rival of Arawn.

Helen of the Hosts: wife of Macsen Wledig.

Herne the Hunter: a spectral horned figure seen riding a stag and leading a hunt. Similar to Gwyn ap Nudd, who leads the Wild Hunt, and Merlin, who rides a stag.

Idris: a giant who likes to sit atop his mountain, Cadair Idris, and star gaze.

Kai: knight of the Round Table and Arthur's seneschal.

Kers-Ys: "city of depths" said to have been swallowed by the sea in the fifth century due to the sins of the citizens.

Kicva: wife of Pryderi.

Kilhwch: suitor of Olwen. Also spelled Culhwch.

Kynon: the knight that first told Owaine of adventure found at the fountain.

Lady of the Fountain: the woman whom Owaine falls in love with on first sight, marries, and guards her miraculous fountain.

Lailoken: a figure similar to Myrddin, whose history has entwined with the tradition of Merlin.

Libane: daughter of King Ecca who neglected her duty to cover a well, which overflowed, drowning the land, to become the waters of Lough Neagh in Ireland.

Llew Llaw Gyffes: "bright one of the skillful hand"; son of Arianrhod and husband of Blodeuwedd.

Llewellyn ap Gruffydd: historic hero of the Welsh.

Lloegyr: land now within the borders of England.

Llyn Tegid: another name for Bala Lake.

Llyn y Morynion: "Lake of Maidens."

Llyr: father of Bran, Branwen, Manawydan, Efnisien, and Nisien.

Lough Neagh: a lake in Ireland said to have drowned the kingdom of King Ecca.

Luned: woman in service of the Lady of the Fountain and friend who helps Owaine.

Mabinogion or Mabinogi: "tales of a hero's childhood." The name given to a collection of tales composed in the thirteenth century or earlier and translated by Lady Charlotte Guest.

Mabon: god of youth.

Mac Beth: eleventh-century king of Scotland whose history contrasts Shakespeare's villain Macbeth.

Macsen Wledig: Magnus Maximus, a Roman from Spain who came to Britain approximately AD 368. In the *Mabinogion* he dreams of and falls in love with Elen or Helen.

Maelgwn: a king of Gwynedd.

Manawydan: son of Llyr; the wise second husband of Rhiannon and equivalent to the Irish sea god Manannan mac Lir.

Math: son of Mathonwy; lord of Gwynedd and great magician; uncle to Gwydion.

Matholwch: Irish king and husband of Branwen.

Merlin: magician and seer-poet who was largely inspired by the historical Welsh bard Myrddin.

Morda: blind attendant of Ceridwen's cauldron.

Mordred: son of King Arthur who (in most versions) challenged his father in the battle of Camlann, where both met their deaths.

Morfan: "great crow"; son of Ceridwen.

Muirgen: "born of the sea"; the baptisimal name of Libane, daughter of Ecca, who lived with her dog in the waters of Lough Neagh.

Myrddin: the Welsh bard whose history Geoffrey of Monmouth drew upon in creating the figure of Merlin.

Nennius (c. AD 800): Welsh monk and historian.

Nisien: "peaceful" or "peace maker"; half brother of Branwen and Bran.

Olwen: daughter of the giant Yspaddaden Penkawr and wife of Kilhwch.

Orddu: witch in Kilhwch and Olwen's tale.

Owaine of the Red Hand: a Welsh hero said to be "sleeping" in a cave with his men, awaiting the need and call of his country.

Owaine: son of Urien of Rheged, who is eventually supplanted into legend and romance.

Pencerdd: "chief of song."

Peredur: the Welsh name for Percivale.

Powys: region of northeast Wales.

Pryderi: son of Pwyll and Rhiannon, and lord of Dyfed.

Pywll: lord of Dyfed, first husband of Rhiannon, and friend of Arawn, who gave him the title "Head of Annwn."

Rheged: the name of the seventh-century kingdom in northern Britain.

Rhiannon: "great queen"; wife of Pwyll and, later, Manawydan.

Seithennin: the notorious drunkard in the tale of the drowning of the kingdom of Cantre'r Gwaelod.

Severn: a river which rises in Powys and flows to the Bristol Channel.

Sleepers: a term used to refer to the popular, widespread tales of native heroes sleeping (in contrast to being dead) in caves, awaiting their country's need.

Sovereignty: a figure that personifies the land.

Suibhne Geilt: an unfortunate, mad, or wood-wild character of Irish tradition.

Taliesin: famed sixth-century historic bard, who also appears in folklore.

Tegid Foel: husband of Ceridwen.

Teirnyon: foster father of Pryderi.

The Triads: a list of traditional Welsh lore and characters grouped in threes.

Tuan Mac Cairill: a figure in Irish tradition who claimed to have shapeshifted to the form of a stag.

Twrch Trwyth: the wild boar featured in Kilhwch and Olwen's tale.

Urien: heroic sixth-century king of Rheged who is praised and made famous by the poetry of the sixth-century bard Taliesin; father of Owain.

Vates: seer-poet.

Wild Hunt: a spectral hunt of men, stags, horses, and hounds that races through the night sky to collect the souls of the dead.

Woodwards: a figure who cares for the wilds, like the Wild Herdsman, as custodian of animals and wild places.

Wood-wild: a term used to refer to the regressed wild nature of "mad" men who lived in the woods with animals, rejecting or rejected by society.

Yns Mons: Isle of Anglesey.

Yspaddaden Penkawr: giant and father of Olwen.

Pronunciation Key

' = appears before stressed syllable
ch = *ck* as in Scottish "loch"
ou = Welsh *aw* as ou in "out"
th = Welsh *dd* as th in "there"
tl = Welsh *ll* as tl in "little"
oo = Welsh *w* as oo in "cook"
u and y = *i* as in "pill"

The spellings of names and places may differ, depending on the source. The pronunciation of some popular figures are as follows:

Bendigeidfran (bendi'gaydfran) / Bran the Blessed

Branwen ('branoowen)

Culhwch ('Kilhooch) / Kilhwch

Custennin (Küs'tenhin)

Efnissien (ev'nissien)

Gwrhyr ('goohrir)

Llew Llaw Gyffes (hlew hlou guff'es)

Llyr (tleer)

Manawydan (man'ouithan)

Matholwch (math'olooch)

Pryderi (pri'deri)

Pwyll ('pooitl)

Rhiannon (hri'annon)

Twrch Trwyth (toorch'trooeeth)

Yspaddaden (usba'thaden)

Bibliography

Aneirin. *The Gododdin*. Steve Short, trans. Llanerch, 1994.

Anglesey Guide to Ancient Monuments. Diane M. Williams, ed. Welsh Historic Monuments, 1989.

Ashe, Geoffrey. *Mythology of the British Isles*. Methuen, 1990.

———. *The Quest for Arthur's Britain*. Paladin, 1968.

Barber, Chris. *Mysterious Wales*. Blorenge Books, 2000.

Berresford Ellis, Peter. *Celtic Women*. Constable, 1995.

———. *Dictionary of Celtic Mythology*. Constable, 1992.

Berti, Giorando and Tiberio Gonard. *Visconti Tarots*. Lo Scarabeo, 2002.

The Black Book of Carmarthen. Merion Pennar, trans. Llanerch, 1989.

Bromwich, Rachel. *Cantre'r Gwaelod and Ker-is, The Early Cultures of North-West Europe*. Cyil Fox and Bruce Dickins, eds. Cambridge University Press, 1950.

Chadwick, Nora. *The Druids*. University of Wales Press, 1997.

Churchill, Winston S. *The Island Race*. Dodd, Mead & Company, 1964.

Cotterell, Arthur. *The Encyclopedia of Mythology*. Acropolis Books, 1996.

Ferguson, Anna-Marie. *A Keeper of Words*. Llewellyn, 1995.

Geoffrey of Monmouth. *Vita Merlini*. Basil Clarke, trans. University of Wales Press, 1973.

———. *History of the Kings of Britain*. Penguin Classics, 1966.

Green, Miranda. *Dictionary of Celtic Myth & Legend*. Thames & Hudson, 1992.

Greer, Mary K. *Tarot for Your Self*. Newcastle, 1984.

Gregory, Donald. *Wales, Land of Mystery and Magic*. Gwasg Carreg Gwalch, 1999.

———. *Wales Before 1536*. Gwasg Carreg Gwalch, 1993.

Griffiths, Anthony. *Snowdonia: Myth and Image*. Y Lolfa Cyf, 1993.

Hollander, Scott. *Tarot for Beginners*. Llewellyn, 1995.

Jarman, A. O. H. and Gwilym Rees Hughes. *A Guide to Welsh Literature, Vol. 1 & 2, 1282–c.1550*. University of Wales Press, 1992.

Johnston, Dafydd. *A Guide to the Literature of Wales*. University of Wales Press, 1994.

Jung, Carl. *The Spirit in Man, Art, and Literature*. R. F .C. Hull, trans. Princeton University Press, 1978.

Kaplan, Stuart. *Encyclopedia of the Tarot, Vol. I & II.* U. S. Games, 1988.

Kendrick, T. D. *The Druids.* Methuen, 1927. Senate, 1994.

Lacy, Norris J., ed. *The Arthurian Encyclopedia.* Peter Bedricks, 1986.

Lofmark, Carl. *Bards and Heroes.* Llanerch, 1989.

———. *A History of the Red Dragon.* Gwasg Carreg Gwalch, 1993.

The Mabinogion. Charlotte Guest, trans. Dover Publications, 1997.

The Mabinogion. Gwyn Jones and Thomas Jones, trans. Dragon's Dream Book, 1982.

Mackenzie, Donald. *Teutonic Myth & Legend.* Gresham Publishing, 1912.

Markale, Jean. *Women of the Celts.* Inner Traditions, 1986.

Matthews, Caitlin. *The Celtic Tradition.* Element, 1991.

———. *King Arthur & the Goddess of the Land.* Inner Traditions, 2002.

———. *Mabon and the Guardians of Celtic Britain.* Inner Traditions, 2002.

Matthews, John. *British & Irish Mythology.* Aquarian, 1988.

Minary, Ruth and Charles Moorman. *An Arthurian Dictionary.* Academy, 1990.

Owen, Elias. *Welsh Folk-Lore.* Llanerch, 1996.

Owen, Wyn Hywel. *Place Names of Wales*. University of Wales Press, 1998.

Piggott, Stuart. *The Druids*. Thames & Hudson, 1968.

Rees, Alwyn and Brinley Rees. *Celtic Heritage Ancient Tradition in Ireland and Wales*. Thames & Hudson, 1961.

Rees, Anthony. *Celtic Legends of Glamorgan*. Llanerch, 1996.

Rhys, John. *Celtic Folklore Welsh and Manx*. Clarendon Press, 1901.

Roberts, Tony. *Castles and Ancient Monuments of West Wales*. Abercastle, 1993.

———. *Myths & Legends of Wales*. Abercastle, 1984.

Rutherford, Ward. *Celtic Lore*. Aquarian Thorsons, 1993.

Senior, Michael. *Gods & Heroes in North Wales*. Gwasg Carreg Gwalch, 1993.

Stewart, R. J. *Celtic Gods Celtic Goddesses*. Blandford, 1990.

Sullivan, K. E. *Scottish Myths & Legends*. Brockhampton Press, 1998.

Taliesin. *Taliesin Poems*. Meirion Pennar, trans. Llanerch, 1988.

Trioedd Ynys Prydein: The Welsh Triads. Rachel Bromwich, ed. Cardiff, 1973.

Thomas, W. Jenkyn. *The Welsh Fairy Book*. University of Wales Press, 1995.

Tolstoy, Nikolai. *Quest for Merlin*. Sceptre, 1985.

Watney, John. *Celtic Wales*. Pitkin Guide, 1997.

Yeats, William. *The Celtic Twilight*. Prism, 1990.

For help in locating Welsh titles, see:

www.gwales.com

Welsh Books Council
Castell Brychan, Aberystwyth
Ceredigion, Wales SY23 2JB

Index

☾ LLEWELLYN ORDERING INFORMATION

 Order Online:
Visit our website at www.llewellyn.com, select your books, and order them on our secure server.

 Order by Phone:
- Call toll-free within the U.S. at 1-877-NEW-WRLD (1-877-639-9753). Call toll-free within Canada at 1-866-NEW-WRLD (1-866-639-9753).
- We accept VISA, MasterCard, and American Express

 Order by Mail:
Send the full price of your order (MN residents add 7% sales tax) in U.S. funds, plus postage & handling to:
Llewellyn Worldwide
2143 Wooddale Drive, Dept. 0-7387-0299-4
Woodbury, MN 55125-2989, U.S.A.

Postage & Handling:
Standard (U.S., Mexico, & Canada). If your order is:
$24.99 and under, add $3.00
$25.00 and over, FREE STANDARD SHIPPING
(Continental U.S. orders ship UPS. AK, HI, PR, & P.O. Boxes ship USPS 1st class. Mex. & Can. ship PMB.)

International Orders:
Surface Mail: For orders of $20.00 or less, add $5 plus $1 per item ordered. For orders of $20.01 and over, add $6 plus $1 per item ordered.

Air Mail:
Books: Postage & Handling is equal to the total retail price of all books in the order.
Non-book items: Add $5 for each item.

Orders are processed within 2 business days.
Please allow for normal shipping time. Postage and handling rates subject to change.

Black Velvet Tarot Bag

100% cotton velvet with purple satin lining and matching drawstring and tassels. Sized to fit large and small decks.

Use this beautifully plush bag to carry and protect any of your treasured oracles: tarot cards, runes and rune cards, Tattwa cards, and more.

0-7387-0208-0 • $12.95

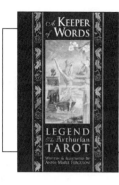

A Keeper of Words

Anna-Marie Ferguson

(Accompanying book to *Legend: The Arthurian Tarot*)

This book is your key to accessing the combined power of two mythic and richly symbolic sources: the 1,500-year-old Arthurian legend and the ancient divinatory system of the tarot.

A *Keeper of Words* first weaves together the fabric of the legend's history and different branches of Arthurian tradition with the symbolic, cultural, and religious aspects of the tarot to clarify the true nature of their interrelationship. It then discusses each card of the *Legend* tarot's major and minor arcana, providing upright and reversed divinatory meanings along with descriptions of the scenes portrayed and their symbolism. This book also retells the Arthurian legend associated with each card and indicates the traditional tarot card to which it corresponds.

1-56718-266-6
276 pp., 6 x 9, illus. • $14.95

4 THE EMPEROR

ARTHUR

1 THE MAGICIAN

MERLIN

ANNA-MARIE FERGUSON

LEGEND
The Arthurian
TAROT

Legend: The Arthurian Tarot

Anna-Marie Ferguson's exquisite watercolor paintings illustrate characters, places, and tales from the Arthurian legends. Each card represents the Arthurian counterpart to the tarot's traditional figures, such as Merlin as the Magician, Morgan la Fay as the Moon, Mordred as the King of Swords, and Arthur as the Emperor.

The Arthurian legend is our strongest and most compelling myth, embodying the romantic ideals of chivalry, bravery and justice, the quest for goodness and truth, the tragedy and ecstasy of love, and the unconquerable spirit's victory over death.

The boxed kit includes a 78-card deck and a 6 x 9, 276-page book, A *Keeper of Words*.

1-56718-267-4 • $34.95

The *Legend Tarot Deck* is available separately.

1-56718-265-8 • $17.95

To order, call 1-877-NEW-WRLD
Prices subject to change without notice

To Write to the Author

If you wish to contact the author or would like more information about this book, please write to the author in care of Llewellyn Worldwide and we will forward your request. Both the author and publisher appreciate hearing from you and learning of your enjoyment of this book and how it has helped you. Llewellyn Worldwide cannot guarantee that every letter written to the author can be answered, but all will be forwarded. Please write to:

Anna-Marie Ferguson
℅ Llewellyn Worldwide
2143 Wooddale Drive, Dept. 0-7387-0299-4
Woodbury, MN 55125-2989, U.S.A.
Please enclose a self-addressed stamped envelope for reply,
or $1.00 to cover costs. If outside U.S.A., enclose
international postal reply coupon.

Many of Llewellyn's authors have websites with additional information and resources. For more information, please visit our website:

WWW.LLEWELLYN.COM